178 SIEGE B/

R.G.A

B.E.F. FRANCE

1916–1918

The Naval & Military Press Ltd

published in association with

FIREPOWER
The Royal Artillery Museum
Woolwich

Published by
The Naval & Military Press Ltd
Unit 10 Ridgewood Industrial Park,
Uckfield, East Sussex,
TN22 5QE England
Tel: +44 (0) 1825 749494
Fax: +44 (0) 1825 765701
www.naval-military-press.com

in association with

FIREPOWER
The Royal Artillery Museum, Woolwich
www.firepower.org.uk

*In reprinting in facsimile from the original, any imperfections are inevitably reproduced
and the quality may fall short of modern type and cartographic standards.*

178 SIEGE BATTERY R.G.A., ALDERSHOT, SEPTEMBER 1916

Officers' Mess

178 Siege Battery

B.E.F. France

Christmas 1918

My Dear May

On behalf of the whole Battery I wish to thank you
and the members of the Committee most heartily for all
the time and trouble you have given to the production
of "A Battery in France."

We all, I hope, shall look back with pleasure on the
days we have spent with " 178," and this book will help
us to keep fresh in our memories the good and bad hours
we have lived through together.

I think our thanks are especially due to the Editor,
whose master hand can be traced on almost every page.

Yours very sincerely

George H. Cooke

EDITOR'S PREFACE

As a result of suggestions made while the Battery was at Fretin in November, 1918, a Book Committee was formed consisting of Lieutenant May (Chairman), Sergeant-Major O'Hara, Sergeant Johnston, Corporals Clench and Thirlwell, Bombardiers R. Boon, T. Whitelaw, I. T. Williams, J. Whitelaw (Sub-Editor), and myself.

Work was commenced at once, and every assistance was given by members of the Battery. The unique nature of such a souvenir was recognised by everyone, and no effort has been spared in the endeavour to make it worthy of the occasion. Any shortcomings will, I hope, be attributed to the circumstances under which the manuscript was written.

A list of all those who have helped to provide material for the book would include more names than could be conveniently printed here, but I have been specially indebted to the members of the Committee, who have always responded willingly to the importunities of the Sub-Editor and myself. My best thanks are here tendered to the two willing typists, Signaller C. Leadbeater and Gunner A. Whitelaw, who have given generously of their spare time ; and I must take this opportunity of acknowledging the permission to reprint "Any Soldier to His Son," kindly given by the Editor of *The Nation* and the author.

J. J. WEBBER

Christmas 1918

PHALEMPIN

CONTENTS

viii

NOMINAL ROLL OF THE ORIGINAL BATTERY

OFFICERS

Capt. J. J. SAUNDERS, 15-9-16 ; 2/Lt. C. JACKSON, 6-7-16 ;
2/Lt. D. K. WILSON, 1-8-16 ; Lt. O. P. NIMMO, 4-8-16 ; 2/Lt.
J. R. JAMIESON, 12-9-16 ; 2/Lt. F. C. FOULSHAM, 10-8-16.

WARRANT OFFICERS, N.C.O.'s AND MEN

B.S.M. M. O'HARA.
B.Q.M.S. A. J. CREIGHTON.
Sgt. J. BLACK.
Sgt. W. MURRAY.
Sgt. T. STEWART.
Sgt. J. JOHNSTON.
Sgt. P. WARDLE.
Staff-Sgt. J. SCULLY.
Cpl. H. HAYES.
Cpl. E. E. BIGGS.
Cpl. T. LAWRIE.
Cpl. J. HASTIE.
Cpl. C. J. P. BREACH.
Cpl. R. NEISH.
Bdr. A. MURRAY.
Bdr. A. GWYNNE.
Bdr. J. ANDERSON.
Bdr. T. S. HENDERSON.
Bdr. A. BENNETT.
Bdr. H. MACNAUGHTON.
Bdr. W. DEMPSEY.
Bdr. J. McLEAN.
Bdr. J. STRANG.
Bdr. E. HAINES.
Bdr. J. S. HANNAN.
Bdr. W. B. GILMOUR.
Bdr. J. BRAIDWOOD.
Bdr. J. GALBRAITH.
Bdr. R. H. DAY.
Gnr. D. B. ALLAN.
Gnr. F. ARMSTRONG.
Gnr. W. H. ARMSTRONG.
Gnr. J. ARNOLD.

Gnr. A. ASHDOWN.
Gnr. A. J. BAIN.
Gnr. W. N. BATES.
Gnr. I. T. BEDDON.
Gnr. P. BONFIELD.
Gnr. R. P. BOON.
Gnr. S. BRINE.
Gnr. A. CALDWELL.
Gnr. F. CAPSTICK.
Gnr. W. CARR.
Gnr. J. CHAPPEL.
Gnr. J. CLARK.
Gnr. T. CLARK.
Gnr. H. CLENCH.
Gnr. R. M. COCHRAN.
Gnr. B. COCKER.
Wheeler C. W. COLE.
Gnr. A. COLEY.
Gnr. F. COOPER.
Gnr. J. H. COOPER.
Gnr. D. CORMACK.
Gnr. J. P. CRAIG.
Gnr. F. CRAWFORD.
Gnr. F. CRAWFORD.
Gnr. R. CUTT.
Gnr. J. DAFFON.
Gnr. B. DALRYMPLE.
Gnr. A. DAVIDSON.
Gnr. J. DAVIS.
Gnr. W. DILKES.
Gnr. A. DODDS.
Gnr. A. E. DUCKWORTH.
Gnr. W. A. FRASER.

B .

NOMINAL ROLL OF THE ORIGINAL BATTERY—*Continued*

Gnr. S. FULLEYLOVE.
Gnr. A. GARVEN.
Gnr. R. GIBB.
Gnr. W. M. GIBB.
Gnr. J. O. GIBSON.
Gnr. J. W. GOSLEY.
Gnr. G. GRAVES.
Gnr. J. GRESHON.
Gnr. D. HALL.
Gnr. J. F. HARVEY.
Gnr. W. B. HENDERSON.
Gnr. J. H. HIRST.
Smith Gnr. E. A. HORNER.
Gnr. H. HORSFALL.
Gnr. C. F. HOY.
Gnr. D. JENKINS.
Gnr. P. JOHNS.
Gnr. O. KIERNAN.
Gnr. J. KING.
Gnr. J. KIRKUP.
Gnr. R. LEACH.
Gnr. A. E. LEWIS.
Gnr. P. LOMAS.
Gnr. A. LOVE.
Gnr. R. McDONALD.
Gnr. J. McGONIGAL.
Gnr. R. R. McGREGOR.
Gnr. A. MITCHELL.
Gnr. J. G. MUIR.
Gnr. J. MUIR.
Gnr. B. MUNDELL.
Gnr. W. A. NEILL.

Gnr. J. S. NIXON.
Gnr. W. NORTH.
Gnr. A. PAIRMAN.
Gnr. J. PARKER.
Gnr. W. H. PARSONS.
Gnr. F. PLOWMAN.
Gnr. F. G. POVEY.
Gnr. D. PRATT.
Gnr. T. J. PRINCE.
Gnr. H. PUNTON.
Gnr. J. R. ROBERTSON.
Gnr. D. B. ROSS.
Gnr. J. F. SCOTT.
Gnr. G. B. SHAW.
Gnr. T. W. H. SHAW.
Gnr. A. T. SMITH.
Gnr. J. M. SMITH.
Gnr. J. STILL.
Gnr. J. STRATH.
Gnr. W. J. S. TAIT.
Gnr. W. THIRLWELL.
Gnr. J. S. THOMPSON.
Gnr. A. WALSHAW.
Gnr. E. C. WALTER.
Gnr. W. WARDELL.
Gnr. C. H. WHITE.
Gnr. J. WHITELAW.
Gnr. T. WHITELAW.
Gnr. D. WILKINSON.
Gnr. D. WOOD.
Gnr. T. WOOD.

OFFICERS WHO HAVE JOINED THE BATTERY SINCE ITS FORMATION.

Capt. G. H. COOKE.
2/Lt. W. CHRISTIE.
2/Lt. H. J. MARSTON.
2/Lt. J. GILL.
2/Lt. A. K. SMITH.
2/Lt. J. A. NICHOLSON.
2/Lt. F. DEWHURST.

2/Lt. S. G. MAY.
2/Lt. F. SHELDON.
Lt. F. S. WEIR.
2/Lt. R. F. PINDER.
2/Lt. H. O. LYDFORD.
2/Lt. E. V. JAMES.
2/Lt. H. L. JOHNSTON, M.C.

ORIGINS

IN the earliest nominal roll of the Battery will be found
the names of men who hailed from various parts of the British
Isles, but among these men were two well-marked groups
each of which had experiences and memories in common.

The Forth R.G.A., a Territorial unit which garrisoned
the defences of the Firth of Forth, provided successive drafts
for the army overseas as our strength in heavy artillery was
increased. Men who had come to know one another while
on the Forth were given the opportunity of joining the
same Battery, and when in June, 1916, Colonel Macmillan
asked for men to join 178 Siege Battery, then in course of
formation, between fifty and sixty names were handed in.

A smaller group of about twenty men was derived from
another source. In the latter part of 1915 drafts of recruits
from the depots at Fort Brockhurst, Yarmouth, and Dover
were sent to join the 49th Company, R.G.A., which formed
part of the garrison on Bere Island, Bantry Bay. They
occupied Fort Rerrin, Fort Ardragh, and Fort Lonehort,
and began the courses of instruction in gunnery and signalling. Some variety was provided in the daily round,
as the island was a station for the examination of shipping,
and signallers took part in the transmission of the necessary
communications. Life on the island was uneventful and
pleasant, though this fact was not fully appreciated until
a few months had been spent in France, and when courses
of instruction were completed a draft for Bexhill bade farewell to Colonel Thrupp, the Y.M.C.A., and the peasantry,
and embarked on the steamer for Bantry, proceeding *via*
Cork and Fishguard to their destination. Life at this lively
watering-place afforded a strong contrast to the Robinson
Crusoe existence of Bere Island, and the troops made the
most of it. On July 20th the original complement of signallers
posted to the Battery left for King's Park, Edinburgh.

Sergeant-Major O'Hara, of the regular army, recalled
from service in France with 4 Siege Battery, and Corporal
Biggs, from 12 Siege Battery, had also reached Edinburgh,
where they were shortly joined by Lieutenant C. Jackson,
of the North Midland R.G.A.

MOBILISATION

Arrangements had been made to accommodate in King's Park the men posted to the Battery, and their first experience provided them with something to write home about. The weather of early July was decidedly pro-German, and the ground put to military uses had been churned into a thick cream. Tent flooring sank gently through the ooze, and pegs refused to stand properly at the slope. The men were now arranged in sub-sections, and after a tiring day sought the shelter of the tents, where the comforts of coast defence accommodation were feelingly remembered. Nor was the wind tempered to the shorn lambs during the night, for a heavy storm burst on the encampment, and the tents, so says my informant, broke away from their moorings and sailed round the park.

On the 6th July a beginning was made with gun drill, and the Battery listened respectfully to the statement that "A detachment for a 6″ howitzer consists of ten gun numbers," and proceeded to carry out the instructions of the drill book on a howitzer represented by two gunners standing like the fore and hind legs of a pantomime elephant. Other apparatus consisted of a blackboard borrowed from Piershill School, a No. 1 director from the R.F.A., 12 semaphore flags from the Boy Scouts, and a buzzer from the camp Adjutant !

A few days later, owing to the tardy return of some members of a neighbouring Battery, an earlier return to camp in the evening was made the rule, but expert local knowledge regarding the wall at Waverley Park enabled the men to avoid any undesirable friction with the authorities on this score.

About the 10th of July, observers', signallers', and layers' classes were formed, and in spite of a lack of modern instruments considerable progress was made in these specialist branches. Corporal Breach and Bombardier Day arrived from Bexhill and joined the observing class, to which they brought particulars of the latest Bexhill methods. About twenty men were selected as signallers, and received

Major J. J. SAUNDERS

instruction in flag-wagging under Bdr. Dempsey at a spot near Holyrood Palace. On the 21st July the Bere Island signallers arrived from Bexhill in charge of Corporal Hayes, and arrangements were made for these trained men to instruct the twenty mentioned above ; but an unexpected visit to the free and easy class at the Y.M.C.A. proved to the officer in charge that the plan would not work.

The ordinary routine was varied by the formation of a concert party, by route marches, and bathing and Church parades. These activities during the last fortnight of the stay were favoured by exceptionally fine weather. On the 26th July an advance party left for Aldershot, and on the 28th the remainder received orders to pack up. Men were allowed out during the afternoon, and arrangements were made for a parade at 8.30 p.m., when the unit would start for the station. In high spirits the Battery numbered off and commenced the march, which to the chagrin of the men drawn from Edinburgh led through the slums. "Are ye gawn tae the front ? " shouted the women standing in the doorways.

At Waverley Station a crowd of sightseers had gathered, and the Battery was overwhelmed with affectionate fare-wells. Finally, amid the usual cheers and yells and waving handkerchiefs, the train pulled out of the station and the tedious journey began. London was at last reached and crossed, train being taken for Aldershot from London Bridge. By this time the "drouth" of some of the party had become acute, and, as carriage doors were locked, it was only by frenzied appeals on behalf of someone who had fainted that a small quantity of water was procured at each station.

On arrival at Ramillies Barracks the sub-sections were allotted quarters, and soon began to take stock of. their surroundings. The first week-end was spent in exploring Aldershot and Farnborough, and on the Sunday morning there was a Church parade at the Garrison Church. Training now began in earnest, with physical drill before breakfast and gun drill on a real 6″ howitzer. Lieuts. Wilson and Nimmo now joined the Battery, and took part in super-intending the work. Among the idiosyncrasies of the officer in charge of the observers was the requirement that they

should, when loaded with apparatus, double off the parade
ground. To the daily delight of the remainder of the
Battery they galloped away with easels, blackboards,
directors, telescopes, and the like, leaping the low hedge
like stags, and disappearing into the fields.

Signallers had now received proper stores, and were
following their craft under the supervision of Lieut. Foulsham.
All work was done with enthusiasm and thoroughness,
and in spare time sport was not neglected. A Battery team
was entered for the Aldershot Swimming Championship,
and against keen competition secured third place and bronze
medals, together with the congratulations of Major-General
Lloyd. The football team, too, was doing well, winning
every match. Week-end passes were easily obtained, and
many men took the opportunity of visiting London, while
others made the most of the local amusements.

Route marches and Church parades saw the Battery
always headed by Gunner D. B. Ross playing the "pipes,"
a custom which both puzzled and amused the public. Con-
certs of the usual type were held, the most successful being
that which took place in Oudenarde Barracks on August
28th. About this time training was sufficiently advanced
for the Battery to hold a field day—a sort of rehearsal in
dummy for the more serious work to follow. The guns were
manned, and a B.C. post, connected by telephone to an
O.P. on Smallshot Hill, was established. Men were stationed
along the Basingstoke Canal with smoke puffs, which were
set off at intervals to represent shell bursts, but by some
mischance the furze caught fire and brought this carefully
staged amateur performance to a premature end. About
a fortnight before leaving Aldershot Lieut. Jamieson joined
the Battery, and a few days later Capt. J. J. Saunders,
who had seen service in France with 109 Heavy Battery,
took over the command. Almost immediately the pro-
cedure of the Battery acquired an air of reality which had
previously been lacking. The guns were hauled about
from one place to another in the fields around the Gun Park,
gun-pits were made and occupied, and the arts of camouflaging, entrenching, and dug-out construction were practised. On September 18th the Battery left for Larkhill,
travelling by rail from Farnborough to Amesbury.

Few soldiers who have been trained in that vicinity show much affection for Salisbury Plain. The dreary march from the station with full pack and equipment almost reached the limits of endurance, and those who needed practice in the army art of " grousing " found ample material in the draughty and leaky huts, the post-office, which for mysterious reasons refused to cash postal orders, and the canteen, which demanded about ten shillings deposit on the knife, fork, and plate required for a shilling supper. After an uncomfortable night in these quarters, the Battery rose at 5 a.m., and proceeded to make a stealthy approach in Indian file towards the position. Here the guns were pulled in, and preparations begun for the day's shoot. After breakfast the novel task of fusing shell was undertaken, and all went well until somebody tried to unscrew a plug which would not budge. The plug was examined first with suspicion and then with alarm. Finally the Staff-Sergeant was left to unscrew the plugs himself.

At last the guns were loaded and ready. " Stand by Number 1." " Fire ! " One-seven-eight had fired its first round. After a fairly successful shoot, the men returned to billets, and during the next few days small parties visited Stonehenge, a couple of miles away, while others acted as guard to a working party of German prisoners. Later in the week Larkhill was startled by the hustling energy of the Battery, which was ordered to commence battery fire at five seconds interval. On the following day an O.P. party was provided for another battery, but realism was carried a bit too far for the tastes of this party when a gun was fired without elevation, and a sudden dash for dug-outs and cover had to be made. After filling in the shell holes, the men returned once more to the billets, and having received the order to pack up, left Larkhill unburdened by regrets and took train for Newbury. At the latter station good spirits came to the surface once more, and dancing to the pipes and singing occupied the interval between arrival and setting off for Stockcross Camp. A march through the dark country lanes brought the Battery to the camp, and after a night's rest the men assembled and drew lots to decide who should be in the first party to go on overseas leave. On Sunday, September 24th, a party consisting of B.Q.M.S.

Creighton and 16 N.C.O.'s and men left for Woolwich to draw battery stores, and an interesting journey down the Thames valley and across London was made, to say nothing of getting a peep at the wonders of the Arsenal and the opportunity of acting the " gay dog " in the evenings. On the return of this party the second batch of men went on leave, while some of those in camp had the novel experience of unloading shell of all calibres from trucks at Newbury Racecourse and being paid for the work by the American firm of contractors. Then the third and last party, mostly Scotsmen, went on leave, and it soon became apparent that the preparations for proceeding overseas were complete.

Evidence of tender and fatherly care was to be found in the fact that every evening each man was detailed to some piquet. There was the Fire Piquet, the Newbury Piquet, the Speen Piquet, and so on, and astonishment was well disguised when they found that their duties led them each evening to the " Dolphin " at Newbury, and necessitated their remaining staunchly on duty there till a late hour. On the 6th of October the party with the guns left camp for Avonmouth, and on the same day the advance party left for Southampton under Lieut. Jackson, but rough weather prevented their crossing until the following evening.

The last night in England, Saturday, October 7th, was celebrated by a fully attended concert at the " Dolphin," where to conclude the proceedings success to the Battery was drunk.

Rising early on Sunday morning, " 178," in full marching order, and headed by the pipes, set out once more for Newbury Station. Farewells were spoken, and the train moved off. Everyone who has marched on to the embarkation platform in khaki knows the thoughts and feelings which then come uppermost, and even the lively strains of the Battery gramophone gave little relief, After lending a hand in loading the mail for France, the men boarded the s.s. *Lydia*, lifebelts were served out, and about 9.30 p.m. the vessel was under way. It was a moonlight night, and on deck the old songs were once more sung before turning in. Dawn next morning found the ship outside Le Havre, and about 7.30 a.m. the Battery disembarked.

ACTIVE SERVICE

ARRAS

On the morning of October 11th, 1916, the guns, stores, and personnel of the Battery entrained at Le Havre for an unknown destination, and after a tedious and uneventful journey in cattle trucks arrived at Savy, a railhead in the Arras sector. The guns were sent to workshop for final overhauling and adjustment, and the men and stores conveyed in motor lorries direct to Dainville. Gun positions had been allotted to the Battery about 800 yards to the right front of the village, the right section on the Arras-Doullens road and the left in a sunken road near the railway station. Billets for officers and men were selected in Dainville, but when a shell hit the sergeants' mess it was decided to remove the men to dug-outs alongside the guns, leaving only the Q.M.S. stores in the village. Later the guns arrived from workshop, and were man-handled into position. Digging parties improved the gun-pits, and made leaky dug-outs more comfortable, and except for the excitement which preceded our first shoot nothing of a special interest occurred during the first week in the line.

The estaminet—Dambrine-Roussel—which was situated in front of the left section, soon became a popular rendezvous for the Battery. Here Germaine, the dainty and gracious young hostess, soon gained our admiration and respect to such an extent that in after days it was counted a misfortune not to have been with the Battery at Dainville. Farmers ploughing the fields in front and behind the guns, civilians walking on the roads near the Battery, and the absence of hostile shell fire occasionally lulled us into the belief that the war had ended. In fact, the only enemies we encountered during those halcyon days were the big grey rats which nightly thronged our sleeping quarters. "Hughie," the three-legged rat, who resided at the left section, might have become a battery mascot had he not ruined all his chances by eating the tasty contents of a gunner's parcel. Spies had been reported in the vicinity of Dainville, and all sentries were warned to keep a sharp look-out. Early one evening the guard was turned out in response to an alarm given by the sentry, who directed them to a disused dug-out, which, he said, had just been entered by some strange individual. The guard, led by an officer with loaded revolver, cautiously approached the entrance, and immediately the light of an electric torch penetrated the darkness a frightened cat leapt into the air, and suspicions vanished in a burst of laughter.

The Battery observation posts—Opera Box and Duchess —which were situated in the reserve trenches, were manned daily by an officer and observers. Observation was more or less a novelty in those days, and the gunners showed considerable interest in the reports brought back from O.P. After a Battery Commander's Post had been completed, and men comfortably installed in good billets, the Battery received orders to move. The completion of the B.C. Post in all future positions proved to be the signal for movement.

On November 12th, 1916—a cold, rainy night—the guns were hauled to a position about a mile along the Arras-Doullens road. Several barns, infested with rats and " chats," were obtained in Berneville for rear billets, and the sleeping quarters around the guns being limited, about 30 men (gunners, signallers, and wireless) slept under the main road in a small tunnel, which nightly resembled a veritable Black Hole of Calcutta. Permanent gun detachments were selected, the remainder of the men being required to dig a B.C. Post and telephone exchange. Shortly after reaching Berneville, Captain J. J. Saunders left for a fourteen days' course in England, while Lieut. O. P. Nimmo went for the same purpose to an artillery school at Hautecloque. Nightly a fatigue party, pulling a trench cart loaded with empty cartridge boxes and petrol cans would leave for Dainville Station to draw the water supply, and many amusing incidents were witnessed when the heavy-laden cart would rest axle-deep in the mud around the guns. The duties of O.C. were taken over by Lieut. C. Jackson, and one morning this officer provided harmless amusement for the Battery and civilians by riding into Corps head-quarters at Arras on a huge, hairy-legged carthorse which he had borrowed for his state visit.

We continued to use our former observation posts, but to obtain a better view of the enemy lines further south we manned an O.P. *de luxe* called " Spaxton," in Beaumetz. Duty at this place was eagerly solicited by observers and signallers, as steak and chips, also beer and *vin blanc*, could be easily obtained at an estaminet scarcely 100 yards down the road. On a clear day the upper storey of this house observation post afforded a view from Arras to the Town Hall at Bapaume.

On December 11th, 1916, the Battery suffered its first casualty. Signaller J. F. Harvey, who had been temporarily attached to the R.E. Signals at Dainville, was killed by a shell which hit the Corps telephone exchange where he was on duty as a telephonist. Signaller Harvey was much admired and respected, and his sad death cast a shadow over officers and men.

Christmas being near at hand, preparations for a good time were made. A concert party was selected, costumes, plum-puddings, cake, whisky, and cigarettes were bought at Avenes to ensure the success of the celebration, and everything promised well. Arrangements had been completed and guests invited, when it was rumoured that a move to another position was probable. At 5 p.m. on December 24th, 1916, the rumour was confirmed, and two hours later, amid loud groans of disappointment, the collecting of stores and pulling out of the guns commenced ; and instead of enjoying a good dinner and concert, we spent Christmas Eve in motor lorries, rumbling along the rough road to Anzin.

After much labour and whisky had been expended, the guns were placed in position near the Arras—St. Pol road by 5 a.m. on Christmas Day. Gun detachments found shelter from pouring rain under gun covers spread out beside the guns. Meanwhile the remainder of the men had been housed in a hayloft in the village of Anzin. The entrance to this abode was negotiated by means of an iron ladder fixed to the outer wall, and as only one man could enter or leave at a time, this furnished many gunners with a good excuse for being late on parade.

Life at Anzin up to the end of the year was more of a routine order, except when the Battery was in action. We had an early parade at 7 a.m., and a Battery parade at 9 a.m., after which Sergeant Wardle, with unconscious humour, would officiate as physical training instructor. Hogmanay and New Year's Day were celebrated by the Scottish element of the Battery in a neighbouring estaminet, where even the forbidding features of the old hag who presided over the establishment could not damp their enjoyment. Her son, who had flaming red hair, answered to the name "Geordie," and the surreptitious manner in which he overcharged the men occasionally brought threats of personal violence on his fiery head. About this time Captain J. J. Saunders was promoted Major of the Battery, and Lieut. O. P. Nimmo succeeded him as Captain. Owing to a number of the gunners suffering from the intense cold, a dose of rum and hot water was now administered at seven each evening, under the supervision of an officer.

On January 5th, 1917, preparations were made by the infantry for a daylight raid on the enemy trenches in front of Arras. This was the first important operation in which the Battery was concerned, and the super-precaution of laying out stretchers beside the guns, and detailing first-aid parties, succeeded in inducing an unnecessary amount of stage fright. At 5.30 a.m. the following morning parties left for the observation posts "Ann," "Eve," and "66," and the bombardment opened a few hours later. The famous 106 fuse, which a number of batteries used that day for the first time, played havoc with the Boche barbed wire. At 3.8 p.m. the infantry went over the top, and after doing considerable damage to the enemy trenches and dugouts with bombs and grenades, they returned with one prisoner—an old, bald-headed individual, who, the "Jocks" suggested, had been purposely left there when the Boche garrison evacuated their shell-swept trenches.

Observation posts were regularly manned after this daylight raid, and it fell to the lot of Signaller A. Ashdown to be the first man in the Battery to climb the chimney

O.P. " Vulcan." The chimney, which was 120 feet in height, stood near Arras station, and commanded excellent observation on the surrounding country. Throughout January and the early days of February, 1917, snow lay on the ground, and movement around the gunpits was not permitted, but each morning the gun teams, in order to keep fit, went for short route marches. A party of men daily left the billets for Dainville to dig gun positions, while others in the Battery were kept busy making camouflage out of newspapers and old shirts to resemble snow. During this spell of exceptionally cold weather, 40° of frost was registered one morning, and a number of men affected by the rigorous conditions were sent to hospital. Gunner Thomson, suffering from acute pneumonia, died at a casualty clearing station after a short illness. His quiet, gentlemanly manner and kind-hearted ways had won him many friends in the Battery.

For strategical purposes certain siege batteries in the Arras sector remained silent, the gunners being employed in making dug-outs and machine gun emplacements in the trenches, but we continued on the active list. One night near the end of January, 1917, an S.O.S. signal was reported to the Battery, and the series of comical incidents associated with this cold night has made it memorable in the Battery history.

On February 18th, 1917, after the customary completion of a B.C. Post and other dug-outs, a working party left Anzin to prepare new gun-pits at St. Nicholas, a suburb of Arras. A few days later the guns arrived, and were placed in an orchard near an *octroi*, from which six roads radiated. Off-duty billets were selected in the Rue de Lille, Arras, and the house, if not shell-proof, was at least dry and comfortable. Several cellars near the guns were also procured for gun detachments and B.C. Post. Estaminets, Y.M.C.A. huts, and concert parties provided ample amusement for the men off duty, and near the end of our stay in the Rue de Lille a piano was " scrounged."

Enemy aerial activity developed considerably in the early days of March, 1917, the Battery witnessing for the first time the destruction of four British artillery planes in one day. From Boche balloons the ever-increasing movement in our lines was being watched, and " Jerry " gunners gave special attention to the traffic continually passing the *octroi* near the Battery position. A gun detachment from the Battery was crossing the square when a shell burst and wounded two infantrymen who walked beside the party, our men being untouched. Some days later Signaller W. Thirlwell hauled a wounded man under cover during a burst of fire, and on March 20th, 1917, Gunner Robertson was wounded near the guns. The following afternoon Fitter-Gunner W. Sutherland was also hit. On the guns ammunition was used at a great rate, and on one occasion the Battery, after expending all its shells, hurriedly despatched a fatigue party to a South African Battery in St. Catherine for further supplies.

The arrival of large consignments of ammunition warned us that the battle of Arras would soon begin, and one night, after unloading 50 lorries of 6-inch shells, we were sent by way of a change to assist in the unloading of another 50 lorries of 9·2's, a task which was only completed about breakfast time next morning. Occasionally the Boche would send over gas shells into Arras, and the mournful church bell would toll the warning to civilians and soldiers in the town. It may be suitably chronicled here that during one of those spasmodic bursts of fire the enemy hit the Battery below the belt when the cookhouse was blown in.

During the next fortnight about 6,000 rounds of ammunition were unloaded and stacked beside the road near the position, for use during the forthcoming battle, and the job of carrying them to the guns over the muddy ground was no light one. We were firing at top speed day and night on counter-battery work, neutralisation, and aeroplane shoots, and all spare men were commandeered to help feed the guns. To ensure uninterrupted communication during the bombardment, armoured cable was buried by the signallers, and a few days later they assisted in the building of a reserve B.C. Post. A party of men under Lieut. F. C. Foulsham then left the Battery to build an observation post south-east of Arras in the trenches evacuated by the Boche some weeks before, and this O.P., which was christened " Twickenham Ferry," needed about ten days' continuous work for completion, and was only occupied by us for the opening day of the battle.

On the morning of April 4th, 1917, the battle of Arras commenced, and after five days' intense bombardment the infantry attacked at daybreak on the morning of the 9th. A forward observation party, consisting of Lieut. Foulsham, Sergeant Hayes, Bombardiers Braidwood and Davis, and Gunners Graves and King, who had left for " Twickenham Ferry " the previous night, early encountered misfortune on the day of the battle. Lieut. Foulsham, acting as forward observation officer, was wounded in the leg by a Boche sniper, necessitating his return to a dressing station, and the party continued under Sergeant Hayes, who shortly afterwards had the unusual experience of taking a prisoner in one of the trenches.

Owing to the guns being out of range at St. Nicholas, orders were received to move up to a previously selected position in Blangy, a shattered village through which ran our front trench systems a few hours before. About 12 noon the guns and personnel passed through the streets of Arras on their way to the new position, and many will remember the strange scenes witnessed on that rough but interesting journey. Boche prisoners straggled down the roads unguarded, while wounded men of both sides gave each other the helping hand. Our aeroplanes hummed continually overhead, diving, twisting, and doing all manner of " stunts." Motor lorries, artillery, ambulances, and relieving battalions of infantry thronged the narrow congested thoroughfares, until the dense mass resembled a giant serpent crawling slowly forward.

Our arrival at Blangy coincided with the arrival of six rounds of shrapnel, which burst just overhead, but this must have been the farewell of some Boche field guns, as no further shell fire was experienced in this village. Guns were drawn off the main road and placed in front of a ruined chateau, and it was not long before the Battery was again in action, engaging the retreating enemy. To hasten the withdrawal, two divisions of cavalry went forward, and no one who was present will forget the fine spectacle of their gallop past the Battery. The only shelters available here were a few water-logged cellars, and to add to our discomfort we now started the three weeks' fast on bully and biscuits. Visual signalling stations were selected, and the signallers did duty at these posts daily.

At 7 p.m. on April 13th, 1917, the Battery moved forward to a position in front of the village of Tilloy, which had been captured by the infantry on the first day of the battle. This being the first time that we had crossed ground previously held by the Boche, everyone showed special interest in the German notices posted on the walls, and it was here we first made the acquaintance of the deep dug-out, a valuable asset during the rough periods of shellfire experienced by the Battery. Under cover of darkness the guns were pulled into position on the crest of some rising ground about a mile in front of Tilloy Wood, but daylight next morning convinced the authorities that the guns were under direct observation from the enemy lines, and about 5 p.m. we withdrew behind the crest. Scarcely had the last gun been removed from the position when the enemy opened fire, and registered a direct hit on the spot where No. 4 stood half an hour before. Sleeping accommodation was found for all the Battery in the deep dug-outs at Chapel Redoubt, and although somewhat foul-smelling, they provided good shelter. Down one of these dug-outs one of the first decorations of the Battery was won by Gunner J. Arnold, who at great personal risk removed a live hand-grenade from a chimney-pipe, thereby saving the lives of a number of men in the dug-out at the time. At the top of the stairway he was wounded in the leg by the explosion of the bomb, but refused to leave the Battery for hospital. For their work in preserving communications during the battle of Arras Sergeant Hayes and Bombardier Haines were also awarded a decoration.

The Boche shelled roads and tracks around the position by day and night without doing much damage, and the open space between the 8-inch battery at our rear and ourselves received special attention, but luckily no one was wounded. Enemy aerial circuses, led by Baron Richthofen

c

in his red and black Fokker, were daily in evidence, searching for unprotected artillery planes or observation balloons, and although night bombing was practically in its infancy, several ammunition dumps in Arras were bombed.

On the guns a friendly rivalry had sprung up between the gun detachments, which accounted for the rapid way the gunners warmed to gunfire at every target. Small corrugated iron shelters were built near the guns, and nightly as we lay listening to the half-hearted burst of the " five-nines " in the mud, many of us speculated as to the chances of a " Blighty." Rations were still limited, and our personal funds soon reached a low ebb owing to frequent visits to canteens and Y.M.C.A.'s for food. The bully beef was palatable to hungry men, but to this day the broken teeth of various members of the Battery bear testimony to the granite-like character of the biscuits we chewed in those lean days. About this time Lieuts. W. Christie and F. C. Marsden joined us, and took over duties as sub-section officers.

Observation parties daily went forward to Orange Hill and the " Brown Line," the journey to and fro being full of incident. On the 22nd of April, 1917, during the attack by the 15th Division on Monchy-le-Preux, Signalling Bombardier James Davis was wounded while acting as telephonist in a trench O.P., and although he was quite conscious when he reached the dressing station, he died a few days later. Bombardier Davis was a popular signaller, and his untimely death was keenly regretted by his many friends in the Battery. The following day E. Haines, another signalling Bombardier, was also wounded while on O.P. duty.

Rifles and belts of ammunition were lying in abundance around the guns and billets, and a slight diversion was provided for the men by establishing a number of rifle ranges near the Battery cook-house. We often whiled away the hours before going on duty by shooting at bottles or bully cans in this home-made shooting gallery. To support the progress of our infantry, on April 30th, 1917, we moved up to a trench position behind the " Brown Line " on the northern side of the village of Wancourt.

The moonlight night and dry weather enabled the F.W.D.'s to draw the guns into position, and the gunners unloaded the stores without difficulty. At dawn next morning we discovered that the guns stood in an open field close to a communication trench, about 500 yards from the main Tilloy-Wancourt road. Dug-outs for B.C. Post and telephone exchange were constructed in the trench, and shelters for the gun detachments also were soon completed.

The weather robbed us of success in the battle of Arras, and there was no lull such as generally follows the completion of a big operation. During the succeeding month heavy tasks of firing were allotted to the Battery, our record day's firing being 1,203 rounds. On the morning of May 3rd, 1917, the enemy shelled the position and vicinity with both gas and high explosive ; and on the same day Signallers J. King and J. Parker, who were on duty at the railway cutting O.P. in front of Wancourt, also had an unpleasant experience. They were seated in a rickety dug-out, which served as a telephonists' room, when a shell burst close to the entrance, burying both men in a heap of sandbags and twisted corrugated iron. Luckily neither of them was injured, although both received a bad shock.

Many will remember the enthusiastic spirit of the genial padre who regularly visited the Battery about this period. Although well advanced in years, he would visit trenches and batteries daily, sometimes carrying a weary soldier's pack, at other times helping a wounded man to the dressing station. We attended his Church services both at the billets and Tilloy Wood, and were all impressed by the courageous example he showed.

On May 15th, 1917, the right section left for a four days' rest, motor lorries carrying the party to an encampment on the ramparts near Dead Man's Corner at Arras, while the left section continued in action, manning two guns. Concert parties of infantry divisions were visited, and a number of men renewed acquaintanceship with their civilian friends in Dainville. The party visited the town of St. Pol on the third day, and spent an enjoyable time far away from the noise of gunfire. On the 19th May they returned to the position, and relieved the gunners of the left section for their holiday. This time Frevent, St. Pol, and Doullens were visited, and everyone seemed to be loud in praise of eggs and chips obtained in the numerous estaminets there. The left section returned to the Battery rested and in good spirits, and settled down once more to life with the guns.

Two days later—May 25th, 1917—a calamity occurred which has never been forgotten by the old members of the battery. About 1.30 p.m. the enemy, who had previously been shelling a 60-pounder to our right front, switched on to our position and dropped a shell between two dug-outs in the trench near the guns. The occupants of the dug-outs, Bombardier W. Gilmore, Fitter-Gunner G. H. Mayes, and Gunner P. Bonfield, were killed instantaneously, while Gunner J. S. Tait died from shock about a day later. Those fine fellows were buried near Arras, the first three at Tilloy Wood and Gunner Tait at Agnez-des-Duissons, the service being read by our old friend, the padre above-mentioned.

It was now decided to move the Battery to the Wancourt Valley, and a party left to prepare the gun-pits. The brilliant sunshine, and the absence of hostile shell fire, contrasted so forcibly with the experiences of the previous two or three months that many of us reckoned those days among the happiest we spent in France. The guns arrived on the night of June 3rd, 1917, and were placed in the gun-pits behind a sheltering bank. Great care was taken to camouflage all traces of footprints or wheel ruts around the guns. Tufts of grass were daily placed over any withered part of the herbage, and men were detailed to water the fresh soil.

Rear billets were moved from Chapel Redoubt, and the Battery took up residence in shelters vacated by an R.E. Company, about 400 yards to the left rear of the guns. The Decauville railway, which skirted the Battery position, was used to bring ammunition to the gun-pits, but it was always necessary that this operation should be done under cover of darkness, and although the artillery duel did not slacken, the splendid weather made our task much easier. About 7 a.m. on the 14th June, 1917, we joined in the barrage which enabled the infantry to capture " Spur " and " Hook " trench, a formidable defence in front of Wancourt. Lieut. Jackson, observing from the railway cutting O.P., kept a careful watch over enemy movement all day, anticipating a counter-attack. About 5 p.m. his vigilance was rewarded when he saw Boche troops concentrating for an attack, and he immediately ordered the guns to open fire. Our Battery, which was the first in action in the sector, landed numerous shells amongst the advancing infantry, who scattered and fled.

On June 24th, 1917, a party of 20 men, under Lieut. Christie, after much speculation had taken place in the Battery as to their ultimate destination, left for Ypres, being followed by the remainder of the Battery about a week later.

YPRES

When the advance party left Arras, the usual rumours were current concerning our early departure for Italy. Some of the men favoured Russia and others Salonika. However, we were destined to visit Ypres, the mention of which will always bring to mind British tenacity. Our forces at this time had defended the salient against repeated fierce attacks by the enemy for over eighteen months, not without huge sacrifices, and it was here that the enemy's advance to the coast was definitely frustrated.

The party, consisting of Lieut. Christie, Sergt. Murray, and 20 men, left Wancourt on the morning of June 24th, 1917, changed lorries at Arras, and then proceeded to St. Pol, where they spent the night. The next day the journey to Ypres was commenced in motor-buses—'buses which at one time had run with their happy loads from Clapham Common to Piccadilly Circus, or from the Bank to Shepherd's Bush. The men arrived at Poperinghe that afternoon, spending the night in a railway shed. The next day a move was made to Vlamertinghe, a village on the main Poperinghe-Ypres road. It was not then badly damaged, and fairly comfortable billets were found in empty houses, where two peaceful days were spent. On June 28th the party marched up to "Asylum Corner" to make the gun positions. A hundred yards further along, on the left of the Ypres road, was the large asylum, badly wrecked, and on the right, some distance away, the ruined gasworks. Due east was Ypres itself. Even at that time the city was only a burnt-out shell, but part of the world-famous Cloth Hall still stood bravely outlined against the sky. Branching off at right angles from the main road to Ypres ran the Dickebush road, along which were some ruined farm buildings. Here the men were billeted, and soon began to make the gun-pits on the eastern side of the road. Many of us who had heard the terrors of Ypres described by old " sweats " in estaminets around Arras at that time had made no secret of our utter disbelief that any place could provide more horrors than Arras. A few days at " Asylum Corner," however, sufficed to alter our opinion. The road junction was shelled every day, and a 6-inch battery to the left rear also received great attention from the enemy's artillery, which knocked out five guns in the ensuing week. Along the rear of our new gun-pits ran a Decauville railway, and it is probable that this helped to draw the enemy's fire. On the whole the advance party received rather a warm time, although only two casualties were incurred, and had it not been for the timely though unexpected arrival of leave warrants, well-attended sick parades might easily have followed. The right section of the Battery, which for four days had been resting near the main Arras—St. Pol road, moved away with two guns on July 1st, stopping for the night at Savy. The next day they entrained and arrived at Abeele late in the afternoon. The guns were almost immediately taken to ordnance workshops for a thorough overhauling after their severe work during the battle of Arras, and the men, after sleeping in the open for the night, proceeded to billets in Vlamertinghe. They then aided the advance party to complete the work on the gun-pits. After one or two journeys from billets to Battery, it was apparent that certain points of the road had been well registered by the enemy. It was soon clearly understood that the cross roads at the edge of Vlamertinghe, the railway crossing a kilometre further on, and "Asylum Corner" should be approached with extreme caution.

It was at this railway crossing on July 6th that Sergt. J. Hayes, M.M., met his fate while proceeding to the Battery. He was severely wounded, and although despatched to hospital with all haste, died the next day. Sergt. Hayes was undoubtedly one of the coolest men under shell fire that the Battery ever had, and the confidence which his men placed in him was a thing to be envied and admired. None of us ever passed this crossing again without being reminded of the loss the Battery had sustained there.

The left section, which had had seven days' rest at Arras while the guns were being overhauled, commenced the journey north on July 9th. Detraining at Proven, they spent the night in a camp near the station, and the following evening brought their guns into the prepared gun-pits, the remaining two guns arriving three days later. We now found ourselves in the thick of it once more, and work proved to be abundant. Judging from the amount of artillery moving up near us, it was evident that another battle was about to take place. The enemy also seemed to have suspicions about our concentration, for he repeatedly swept known and possible battery positions. Ours was no exception, and " Take cover ! " was a very frequent order. On July 13th the enemy heavily bombarded Ypres and the surrounding district with gas shells containing a new gas, causing many casualties. Our men, however, received the warning in time, and, donning their box respirators, escaped harm. Two days later one of the cooks, Gunner J. Still, was wounded in the head by shrapnel.

The gun telephone dug-out behind the position was a small place of iron and concrete, built inside a ruined barn—splinter-proof, but no more. This, however, was the only shelter to which we could run when heavily shelled. On July 18th a heavy concentration was put on the Battery position, and, the men not being in action, ran as usual for this dug-out. Shells rained all around the flimsy structure, and one, bursting near the door, killed Gunner Henderson and wounded three others. " Chicken," as he was popularly called, was a genial young Scotsman and a good sport, whose cheery voice was greatly missed in the Battery. At his funeral we discovered by chance, on looking at one of the memorial crosses, that Sergt. Breach, who left us at Arras, had also been killed in action. A little over a week later a similar incident occurred, and Gunner Moffatt was killed and Gunner Lomas wounded near the right section. It was here that Gunner Muir earned his Military Medal and Gunners Garven and Walter their Croix-de-Guerre, for dashing out into a hurricane of shell fire to render first aid to the unfortunate men. Gunner Moffatt had been with the Battery only a short time, but he had made many friends who greatly regretted his death.

During the period from July 21st to the last day of the month a more or less continual bombardment was maintained on the enemy's trenches, batteries, and lines of communication. Thousands of rounds of ammunition arrived at the Battery position, and were as quickly disposed of. On the first day of the bombardment over twelve hundred rounds were fired by the four guns, and a few days later one gun delivered to Fritz more than three hundred and sixty " iron rations." As all the other batteries in the neighbourhood were doing similar good work, a rough idea can be obtained of our preliminary bombardment for the third battle of Ypres. Preceded by a barrage which opened at 3.45 a.m. on July 31st, our infantry went over the top. The enemy was evidently prepared, for almost immediately he returned a heavy fire, mostly on our trenches, but our gallant divisions, undeterred, went forward to capture the " Black Line," an advance of about six thousand yards. The ground over which they had to pass was a most difficult stretch of country, including well-defended trenches, thick belts of barbed wire, several " pill-boxes," and Hill 35. By midday it was reported that all our objectives had been gained, and our wounded returning from the grim struggle were very cheerful and pleased with their morning's work. Our guns then slackened, keeping up only a protective barrage at a slow rate of fire. About 5 p.m. the enemy heavily counter-attacked. S.O.S. rockets immediately soared into the air, and the gunfire increased in volume. Our infantry, despite desperate fighting, were forced to relinquish their hold on Hill 35, Gallipoli Farm, and Hibernian Farm. These two so-called farms were the largest and strongest " pill-boxes " in the enemy's system of defence, and they proved great obstacles in our subsequent operations. Some of our signallers went forward with the Brigade Observation Party, and had a very warm time indeed. They followed the infantry over the top, and eventually established themselves in Plum Farm and Apple Villa, which they were forced to leave hurriedly on account of the enemy's counter-attack.

The month of August proved to be very wet ; the ground soon became a morass, and we very quickly realised the unique character of Flanders mud. Artillery duels continued to be frequent, and several attacks and counter-attacks took place during the month. The terrible condition of the ground, however, prevented any big advance being made, but Langemarck was captured on August 16th. When the weather permitted our airmen were very active, and we were interested witnesses of many air-fights. In

one case a venturesome Hun " fighter " attacked a " B.E."
plane just above the left section guns.   We were beginning
to feel genuinely sorry for our airman, for he was forced
lower and lower in spirals.   Machine bullets pattered into
the gun-pits, and we began to think about the danger to
ourselves, when, riddled by a sudden upward burst of fire,
the enemy plane crashed to the ground amidst cheers from
the onlookers.

The Battery moved forward on August 24th to a position
known to us as " The Vinery."   It was a particularly hard
night's work, for the guns had to be man-handled some distance over shell-pitted ground, both in pulling out and in
pulling in.   However, about 5 a.m. the next morning we
succeeded in getting the last gun into position, and then
commenced to disguise them with camouflage.   When it
became sufficiently light we surveyed the surrounding
country.   Directly in front of us was a ruined farm—" The
Vinery "—where our old second line ran, and about half
a mile to the rear were the remains of the village of St. Jean.
To our right flank was the " White Chateau," and further
south the village of Potyze.   We decided that on the whole
it was quite a good position, for there was a deep sap in the
trench in front of the guns, and farther forward a sufficiently
large wood to screen the gun-flashes.   The nearest road was
about four hundred yards away, but the difficulty of bringing
up ammunition was overcome by using the Decauville
railway, which ran past the left flank of the Battery.   Only
one field battery could be seen in front of us, and a day or
two later it was forced to seek a fresh position to our rear
owing to heavy enemy shelling.   We suffered four light
casualties during the next two days, two of which were
caused by aeroplane bombs.   Day and night bombing
became rather a favourite pastime of the enemy during the
following period, and nothing less than 20 feet of earth
overhead gave that feeling of security so necessary for
peaceful sleep.   On August 27th another attack was made,
in which Hill 37 was captured.   We had been working hard
the previous night, carrying ammunition and fusing shells,
and very early in the morning the barrage started.   Seven
prematures from the field guns behind burst in as many
minutes over our heads, and splinters from the enemy's

shells began whistling about. We could not hear one another speak on account of the deafening noise, and orders were given on the guns by waving the arms, the section commanders using semaphore. Despite these difficulties, however, we kept up the gunfire at a fast rate.

After an hour or so orders came through for a slower rate of fire, and we maintained a fairly heavy bombardment on the enemy well into 'the evening. Meals were snatched by allowing only one man of a gun team to run to the cookhouse and hurriedly swallow his food. After replenishing the stock of ammunition near the guns, the men turned in late at night for a few hours' sleep. They proved to be very few indeed, for we were turned out five times in response to S.O.S. rockets sent up by our infantry, and once to unload a thousand rounds of ammunition. Naturally everyone grumbled and swore horribly, but after all very little has been done in Flanders without the abundant use of bad language.

There followed a period of as hard work as we had ever experienced. Luckily the weather had improved, making things much more bearable. Day after day the reliefs on the guns changed, and hundreds of rounds of ammunition were used up. An aeroplane shoot of about three hundred rounds, beginning as soon as visibility was sufficiently good, was almost a daily happening. The reliefs reached the Battery position by entering Ypres, turning to the left before reaching the Cloth Hall, and then wending their way up No. 4 or No. 5 track. The mention of these tracks, particularly the former, will make certain members of the Battery shiver even now. In bad places duckboards had been laid, and the remainder of the track across the fields had been so well worn that its position could not be hidden from the enemy. Consequently it came in for very nearly as much attention from the Boche guns as the Potyze road. The customary practice of marching in small bodies of ten men separated by an interval of one hundred yards was rigidly carried out in our perilous journeys to and from the Battery position. It was really wonderful to see how eager the men were to go on duty if the shells were falling behind them. On No. 4 track the tragedy of the missing D3 telephones was enacted. The situation being rather unhealthy one day, our worthy ration orderly was only too glad to dump the rations and stores at the side of the track and seek cooler climes. The men on duty, after pondering on the prospects of salving the load, decided that life was sweet even without rations, and some undiscovered hero " lifted " the D3's. An immortal song was composed by one of our tame poets on this episode.

During the week following the attack on August 27th four more men were wounded in the Battery position. Considering the number of times the enemy. shelled our vicinity the casualties we received were wonderfully few, but our artillery was packed so closely that one battery often suffered from " strafing " intended for others. We had learned the value of deep saps at Arras, and were very grateful for the near presence of the one in front of the guns. We found that in Belgium it was not possible to dig any considerable depth without striking water, and it was there-fore necessary to pump this dug-out clear every day and night. The hosepipe which brought the water upstairs and into the trench being rather leaky, the steps were always treacherously slippery, and when the order " Take cover " was given, the men slid rather than ran down the steps. The chamber at the bottom was divided into several small compartments, and the roof, sides, and floor of these were always wet. Despite the gloomy atmosphere down below, we felt decidedly safer under the continual drip of water from the roof than in the fresh air above, where we were in constant danger.

On September 11th misfortune again overtook us, for Corporal Braidwood, who had done such good work as an observer before returning to duty on the guns, was killed by a 4·2 shell near No. 1 gun-pit. The severeness of the loss was apparent from the numerous downcast faces in the Battery that day, and everyone who could possibly be spared attended his funeral to pay their last tribute to the dead. Our ill-luck had not ceased, however, for the same night, when No. 4 gun was being brought back from work-shops after having been repaired, Fritz heavily shelled the area with mustard-gas shells. The immediate effect of the gas was not severe, and, ignoring it, we proceeded with the task of pulling the gun into position again. Some difficulty was experienced in fitting the girdles on the gun-wheels,

and it was five or six hours later when the relief on duty
turned in, the men off duty who had been brought up to
assist returning to their billets at "Asylum Corner." It
was almost midday on the morrow before the ill-effects from
the gas were felt by any of the men, and then their aching
eyes and throats warned them that the facetious person
who, the previous night, had voiced the opinion that Fritz
meant no harm had strayed sadly from the truth. Before
nightfall about 40 N.C.O.'s and men had been admitted
into hospital " gassed," and as a party of 12 men had been
sent to Boulogne a week previously to recruit their health,
six gunners were all that could be mustered to man the four
guns. This unfortunate band of heroes, some of them
suffering severely from inflamed eyes and throats, were
condemned to continual duty for six days and nights before
reinforcements arrived from the base depot. The remainder
of the month of September saw a continuance of our heavy
bombardments, and some of the reinforcements who had
just arrived in the country for the first time were not long
in making acquaintance with hard work and severe shelling.
On October 4th a successful attack was launched on Brood-
seinde. A 9·2 battery which had pulled in on our immediate
left front the previous night, and had not had time to erect
camouflage over the guns, must have been observed early
in the fight, for the enemy commenced counter-battery
work on it. A lucky, or unlucky shell, according to the
point of view, dropped amongst the ammunition on one
of the gun-floors, and in a second projectiles weighing two
hundred and eighty pounds flew in all directions. The
unfortunate battery—66 S.B.—suffered severely, and the
splinters and falling shells drove our men to cover. Despite
the danger, however, some of them rushed to render first
aid to the wounded. On the same day a sigh of relief was
heaved by us all when it was announced that 15 S.B.,
having enjoyed a comparatively easy time for some months
on the Somme, were to take over the right section guns.
That night the men went off duty with a light heart, knowing
that in all probability they were soon leaving Ypres and all
its terrors. Even the left section relief coming on duty
looked surprisingly cheerful, for they were anticipating
the time when they could follow their luckier comrades.

Their faces fell somewhat, however, when a rumour became current that a further move forward was imminent.   This rumour, unlike so many others of its kind, proved to have truth for its foundation, and the next day " caterpillars " arrived to pull the guns out.   We proceeded up the Zonne-beke road, passing the junction formed by Oxford and Cambridge roads, and then turned off to the right, pulling into position on the western slopes of Frezenberg Ridge.

Even the "caterpillars " had great difficulty in pulling the guns along the track from the road to the gun-pits just vacated by the Australian Field Artillery, for the mud was, in places, two feet deep.   All around us lay a scene of desolation.   The German trenches, concrete shelters, and barbed wire had been broken and twisted until the ground was disfigured beyond description.   Bad weather had set in again, and every shell-hole was full of evil-smelling water.   Here the problem of making good shelters for the men was never solved, but a ramshackle cook-house was made in a trench behind the guns, and the detachments made the best of the very poor dug-outs near the gun-pits. It had been deemed inadvisable to move the billets from "Asylum Corner," for east of Ypres the terrific shell fire had worked such havoc that there was hardly rain-proof cover for a mouse.   This necessitated a very long walk from billets to the position, and the road being unhealthy in more than one sense, the numberless duckboard tracks were used.   There seemed to be one of these tracks for every letter of the alphabet, many of them starting pro-misingly and ending in a quagmire.   One of our sergeants, thinking himself an expert in these matters, led his detach-ment down each in turn from "A" track to " Z " track, but none seemed to lead in the right direction, and we generally had to desert the duckboards and make a bee-line for that prominent landmark—the Cloth Hall.   It surprised many of us to find how easily we could become lost when only a few hundred yards from the position.   Men would leave the guns for the cook-house, and in a short time, glaring savagely at the landscape in all directions, would wonder where on earth they were.   A whole relief lost its way one night, and it was only after waiting three hours that the men, eagerly looking forward to their turn for rest, heard wild shouting for " 178." At Frezenburg we carried on under great difficulties, for after firing ten rounds per gun hours had to be spent in freeing the trail from the clinging embrace of the mud and patching up the platforms. It was bitterly suggested by a No. 1 that the instructors who taught N.C.O.'s to build platforms at Bexhill would do well to try their theories in this interesting locality. The enemy's artillery must have been in a similar plight, and very few shells burst near us, although the valley beneath was a scene of constant movement. It was up the track behind the guns that the pack-horses and mules came, laden with ammunition for the Field Artillery. Wading knee-deep, the drivers urged the animals along, but often a poor beast, sinking up to the withers, would have to be shot and abandoned. Luckily this nightmare of mud ended on October 14th, when the remainder of 15 S.B. arrived to relieve us.

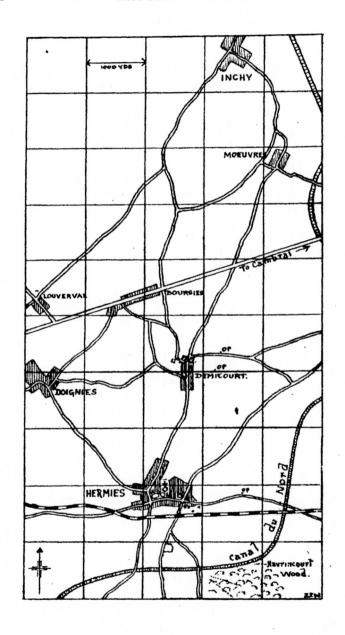

CAMBRAI

There was a remarkable heartiness and vigour about the singing of the old songs as the Battery column rattled down the road to Poperinghe. The feeling of relief at leaving Ypres was so great that even the military police were waved a gracious farewell over the tailboard. Yet some of the men were not so fortunate, and, as related above, did not leave Frezenburg until October 14th, to follow the advance party. Meanwhile the latter had reached Arras, and was billeted for a night in the cheerless basement of a large school or college not far from the station. There was hardly time to recall the incidents and adventures of the previous stay in this district before the party was once more on the road for Wancourt. Here the comfortable dug-outs occupied during the summer had fallen into other hands, so that it was necessary to make the best of some deserted dug-outs in the chalky soil, and before long the settlement was completed. On the 8th October the guns of 15 Siege Battery were handed over. It was a night of pitch darkness and pelting rain, and the ground round the old position which we were to re-occupy was only practicable for " caterpillars." The weird sight of these monsters rearing up and side-stepping in the light of the torches will not readily be forgotten. As No. 3 ran into the gun-pit an unfortunate accident occurred ; the trail, swerving sharply, struck Gunner Leverick, who was standing near, and broke his leg.

Wancourt proved to be a " soft cap " position, for though inquisitive Boche planes were constantly on the prowl, we were unmolested by the enemy during the three weeks of our stay. On Sunday, 14th October, we were allotted a bombardment task in connection with a raid made by the Argyll and Sutherland Highlanders. After steady firing from morning onwards the rate quickened between 4 and 5 p.m., when the infantry went over the top and successfully completed the operation. During the day the firing of the 15-inch howitzer, No. 10 R.M.A., was watched with interest, as it was possible to follow with the

D

eye for a great distance the flight of the 1,400 lb. projectile.

Having made the dug-outs comfortable, and being favoured with a very rainy night—two indispensable conditions for a regulation shift—the Battery pulled out and proceeded farther south to St. Leger, which was reached on October 29th, after a pause of three days at Agny. As far as warfare was concerned, the conditions remained much the same as at Wancourt, and apart from some calibration shoots, nothing of importance occurred on the guns. `

After some days spent in making and re-making dug-outs, a more or less regular routine began. The relief off duty spent the time in billets at St. Leger itself, some twenty minutes' walk from the Battery, being marched up each morning to join the relief on duty for a few hours' foot drill, musketry, and gas mask practice. In the afternoon a short course of interesting lectures on gunnery and map reading was given to N.C.O.'s and B.C.A.'s by Captain Cooke and Lieut. Jackson. The Battery telephone exchange provided a certain amount of amusement at this position. The code message indicating that a Boche working party needed attention was " Boiled beef and carrots " ; another code message was " Mixed bathing," while the O.P.'s rejoiced in such names as Mabel Love, Gertie Millar, and Jenny Lind. The bewilderment of a telephonist who had not been warned of the prevailing type of humour was a joy to behold.

Our ultimate destination lay still farther south, and the pauses at Wancourt and St. Leger appear to have been a device for masking our approach to the Cambrai front. On the night of November 14th we pulled out once more, and were soon on our way *via* Bapaume to Ytres, where we arrived about daybreak. Having had breakfast, we then found an opportunity of getting a few hours' sleep on the floor of the Nissen huts in which we had taken shelter, but in the afternoon all men were sent to the railway station, where guns and stores were loaded on the Decauville trucks. At dusk one party started on foot for billets at Neuville, the other party going by train with the guns to the new position. Unloading the guns at a point on the edge of Havrincourt Wood was the first problem. Little light could be used owing to the danger of enemy observation, and following on the bad weather the ground, except where

a few logs had been laid down, was a perfect quagmire.
Running north-east from the railway was a sunken road,
in the bank of which the pits and dug-outs, previously
occupied by another battery, were situated. The guns were
man-handled down this road, but the task of manœuvring
them into position over the slimy mud and chalk was un-
usually difficult ; the wheels threatened to sink axle deep,
and only after hours of pulling on the ropes were the detachments able to break off for a rest in the early morning.
Ample cover was available in the deep dug-out, which could
be reached by a stairway entered from the gun-pit, and every
care was taken to guard the secrecy which was the great
characteristic of the preparations. To keep telephonic
communication ' on the sector about normal, the newly-
arrived units sent and received messages by despatch rider
only. The line, though laid, was not connected up to the
instruments, so that no unusual activity could be detected
by the Boche listening sets. This gave rise to an army
rumour which has become a Battery classic. The Boche,
so the newsmonger said, was to be attacked by a method
which was both effective and novel. An electric wave of
unparalleled intensity was to be projected from our lines,
all instruments in the enemy lines were to be put out of
order, and owing to the terrific magnetism developed every
rifle and gun would jam at the critical moment and the
victory would be ours !

Unending lines of transport and troops passed along
the roads under cover of night. Ruyalcourt swarmed
with troops, who marched in under cover of darkness, and
no hint of this concentration reached the enemy. The
night before the attack saw a long line of big tanks drawn
up on the borders of the wood, each having the great faggot
for trench crossing fastened aloft. Arrangements for visual
communication during the battle were made, and a party
consisting of Corpl. Graves, Bdr. Thirlwell, Signallers
Walshaw, Macgregor, Hull, Brine, Povey, King, and Kiernan,
left Neuville late on the afternoon of the 19th to take up
a position at an O.P. on the eastern edge of the wood,
where they were joined later by Lieut. Christie. To the
same spot came a party of men from 277 Siege Battery,
and arrangements were made for this party to follow up

when the attack had made some progress, keeping in communication meanwhile with our station at the O.P., either by 'phone or visual. During the night the rattle of the tanks advancing to take up position could be heard on all sides, and more than once the line needed repairing as a result. Towards morning the enemy put down a heavy trench mortar barrage. At 5.50 a.m. the lines were connected to the instruments, and half an hour later the moment for the great surprise arrived. The enemy was quite unprepared. It had been customary, so a prisoner said, to put troops from Ypres and other active sectors into this part of the line for a rest. To our tremendous opening barrage of high explosive, shrapnel, and liquid fire the enemy made a feeble reply, and apparently evacuated his front line in panic.

Meanwhile the forward party mentioned above had left the O.P., and were going towards the line reeling out cable, but after speaking over the 'phone once, they gave no further sign. Signaller Macgregor was then sent forward along the line to discover what had happened. He found that the line of advance was under sniping fire, and it was only after a risky journey through and over the trenches that he came to what had been the No Man's Land of the day before. Here he found the party taking cover in a shell-hole, a Bombardier having been killed and another man wounded.

About 9 a.m. two signallers, King and Kiernan, taking with them a signalling lamp, went forward in search of information. Passing across our front line into No Man's Land they followed the track of the tanks through the great stretches of enemy wire and reached the Hindenburg line outposts. It was evident that in taking these our casualties had been very slight. Still following the tank route they then came to the main Hindenburg line, which fully bore out all that had been related concerning it in the papers. There were recesses and stores for all materials, thick concrete overhead cover, ample provision of deep dug-outs, telephone exchanges, and officers' quarters. Everything was spick and span. In the dug-outs was evidence of a hurried departure ; cigars, rum, black bread, clothes, and equipment were all left behind, and what was perhaps the most surprising find, plenty of clean ironed underclothing. Stoves there were in plenty, together with firewood. The return journey was made *via* Havrincourt village, and here news was obtained that the 62nd Yorkshire Division had gained the second objective, and that the cavalry were on the move. A German canteen in the village stood invitingly open, but it was found that those very thorough fellows, the British Infantry, had not omitted to " mop up."

As is well known, the Cambrai attack was successful on the right but was held up before Mœuvres and Bourlon on the left. To support a further attack in that direction artillery was brought up into Demicourt, a small village about 1,500 yards from the line, and we prepared for a bombardment which opened at 10.30 a.m. on the 23rd November. The billets were now situated in Hermies, where stables and pig-sties were cleaned out and made more or less habitable. The proverbial good luck of the Battery failed for a moment in this village, for it was a neighbouring unit that found the buried wine-cellar, and their subsequent task of wiring in No Man's Land was done with surprising gusto.

Little of note occurred during the first few days at Demicourt, though the conditions there were not at all reassuring. From behind the battery position our own bursts' could be observed, and at night the Véry lights appeared to be going up in the rear as well as in the front, the usual phenomenon of a salient. There was little cover for the detachments among the ruined houses at the forked roads, and No. 4 gun in particular occupied a very open position. Our first casualty here was Gunner Preston, wounded near No. 2 gun on the 27th. The B.C. Post was a stable situated close beside the main road, which ran in a northerly direction through the village. It had an improvised roof made of loose pieces of corrugated iron and a gun-cover. By the 28th the enemy had apparently brought up more artillery, and on that night the communications were constantly cut, the roof of the B.C. Post lifted, and the signalling stores in the adjoining shed struck. Soon after midnight it was decided to adjourn to the field in which the O.P. was situated, about 300 yards to the east, but as by some weird chance the enemy immediately

" bracketed " on the party, it was not long before a return was made to the stable. The next day passed fairly quietly, but the detachments which relieved about 5 p.m. that afternoon were destined to undergo a severe trial.

The first indication of an attack on the 30th was a heavy trench mortar bombardment on our right front, at 6 a.m., and about half an hour later the first shell burst on the road near the B.C. Post. All communications were soon broken, and as the situation was obviously critical the Battery was immediately ordered to open fire on S.O.S. targets. Enemy fire slackened about 8 a.m., and the men managed to snatch a hasty breakfast. From nine o'clock onwards the intense bombardment was resumed, and it was with great difficulty that our guns kept in action. The nervous strain was beginning to tell, and just before 11 a.m. the detachments had been driven to cover by the accurate firing of the enemy. About this time Lieutenants Smith and Dewhurst were relieved by Lieutenants Jamieson and Sheldon, who were accompanied by Captain Cooke (then acting O.C.). The latter immediately went to the guns, and, setting a fine example of coolness and bravery, soon restored confidence. The enemy replied vigorously to our fire, round for round, and later on, when a shell burst almost under the muzzle of No. 4, the detachment was ordered to take cover in the dug-out. The men had scarcely got inside when a shell burst at the entrance, wounding Bdr. Eckersley, Gunner Craig, and Gunner Irving. Every attention was given to the wounded men by their comrades, assisted by the Captain, but Irving, to our great regret, died in hospital. Shortly after this had occurred Gunner Lambourne, who had been helping on No. 4 gun, left this shelter to return to the dug-out of No. 1 gun, but being seriously wounded on the way he came back again, and after receiving the best attention possible under the circumstances, was taken to hospital, where he, too, died some days later.

Between 12 and 2 o'clock heavy gas shelling was experienced, and few of the men were able to get to the cook-house for dinner. Later still a Boche plane, flying low, subjected the detachments to machine gun fire, and it was about this time that a shell blew away the corrugated sheeting that sheltered the wireless apparatus, and half buried

Bdr. Clark, Wheeler Cole, Gunner Bates, and Gunner Hannan. The aerial of the wireless station was snapped, and after repeated attempts, was repaired by Signaller Cocker, assistant wireless operator. The cook-house fared no better than the above places, and the work there was carried on under great difficulties. As so few men had been able to come for dinner, Jimmy Ash, the cook, had prepared some rice for tea, but a well-placed shell flung bricks and brickdust into the dixie of rice, and in humorous despair Jimmy made his famous threat, " If Jerry don't soon stop this, I'll put half a dozen loaves in a sandbag and go over and give myself up."

The same night the Battery pulled out, being favoured by a lull in the enemy activity, during which gun stores and signalling stores were rapidly loaded and sent back to a new position at Hermies. Associated with Demicourt is another incident which occurred a few days later. Lieut. May, with two signallers, was on duty in the little semi-circular trench O.P. to the right of Demicourt, on December 3rd. About midday the line was broken, and one signaller went out to mend it. Not long after this shells began to fall in the vicinity of the trench at the rate of one per minute, and as the position was isolated and open it seemed certain that this was an observed shoot. The officer and signaller now moved about nine or ten yards along to a narrower portion of the trench, and immediately a shell struck the covered end just vacated, destroying director and telephone, as well as the overcoats, gas masks, and rations of the party. A lightning sprint, probably viewed with great satisfaction by a Boche observer, was then made for the village, and when the O.P. was examined about an hour later it was found that five direct hits had been obtained on the short piece of trench.

Hermies, which occupies so large a place in this story, was in some ways a remarkable village. From the great heap of stones which marked the site of the church a fine view could be obtained of the undulating country stretching away below. Due north lay Demicourt and Boursies, and to the left of them the village of Doignies. Five miles away, on the high ground behind Demicourt, stood Inchy, with Mœuvres a mile and a half nearer Hermies, and a little more to the right as seen from the church. To the north-east stood out plainly the dark mass of Bourlon Wood. Close by Hermies church was the entrance to the catacombs, a huge cavern which would accommodate 400 men, and not a stone's throw from this entrance was a huge mine crater having a circumference of close upon 200 yards. A slightly smaller crater, in the bottom of which some enterprising Tommies had built a hut, was situated near the cross-roads at the eastern end of the village. Along the southern edge of the village ran the railway, and a thousand yards farther south the unfinished Canal du Nord. Between the village and the railway was the new battery position, and just beyond the southern bank of the canal were the billets. The B.C. Post was a disused dressing station, and here in the afternoons Major Saunders, fresh from a course in England, lectured on the latest methods in artillery work to the officers and B.C.A.'s of the Battery.

Winter was now upon us, and the miserable little shacks by the canal afforded little comfort. Spasmodic shelling of the roads and canal made the journey to and from the Battery rather exciting at times, and towards the end of the month Gunner Daniel Jones was wounded by a shell which struck a dug-out one night at the Battery. Christmas Day was celebrated with beefsteak and plum-pudding, together with the cup that cheers. With leave warrants coming in regularly and little artillery activity on either side the New Year was hopefully welcomed. During the next few days, however, the situation was decidedly " jumpy," and there were frequent orders to fire on S.O.S. targets ; but all speculations as to the plans of the enemy were cut short by the welcome intimation that the Battery was to go out on rest to Beauval, the first genuine rest since arriving in France. Sunday, January 6th, was a frosty day, and the snow still covered the ground, so that transferring the stores and baggage across the canal was no small task. The southern bank was steep and slippery, next came the narrow temporary footbridge, and then the glassy steps by which the top of the northern bank was gained. At the Battery similar difficulties were experienced, a slight downfall of rain having made the road surface almost impracticable for heavy traffic, but skid chains and patience solved the problem, and at 5 a.m. on the Monday morning we left the village.

BEAUVAL AND GOUZEAUCOURT

On the first day we passed through Ytres, Etricourt, and Manancourt, then turning to the north-west at Clery we reached in the evening the village of Maricourt. The weather was still wintry, and more than once during the day it was necessary to assist the F.W.D.'s with man-power and drag-ropes. A great shed with at least 200 wire beds fitted up in it was allotted to the Battery for the night, and the number of men under one roof was probably a Battery record. At 7 a.m. the next morning we marched off along the frosty roads to the lorries, slung the kits aboard, and set off again. The country through which we passed was well wooded, and the wintry landscape became less dreary as we went along. At intervals we dismounted from the lorries to haul at the drag-ropes or to run a short distance for the sake of warmth. About midday a blizzard swept across the country, making progress still more difficult. Albert was reached about one o'clock, and here a search was at once made for food and drink. One experienced " scrounger " wandering into a courtyard found an army cook-house fully staffed, with ample supplies of hot roast beef, vegetables, bread, " duff," and boiled rice, and to his great surprise was told by the cooks that only guests were lacking. The ability of the Battery to adapt itself to unusual circumstances was instantly shown, the subsequent operations being carried out with complete satisfaction to all concerned.

Leaving Albert we passed through Bouzincourt, and soon came to our next stopping-place, Forceville, the first village uninjured by shell fire that we had seen for many a day. The village church, the houses and streets, all covered with snow, stood out plainly on this clear starry night. Gleams of light shone from the cottage windows, and down the main road passed the motor-cars with brilliant lamps. We stayed for the night in cheerless barns, and were not sorry to leave them in the early morning, when after some difficulty in starting up, the journey was resumed *via* Acheux, Vauchelle-Authie, and Louvencourt. On this

occasion a proper midday meal was out of the question, but
we made a fairly good feed on anticipation and raisins,
and after more rough weather passed Doullens, stopped at
an estaminet, and then entered Beauval in a driving snow-
storm late in the afternoon of the 9th of January. Billets
were found in the barns of this agricultural village, and
investigations soon proved that we had come into a land
flowing with milk and coffee, to say nothing of eggs and
chips. A thaw soon set in, and our morning programme
generally included gun drill, musketry, foot drill, and route
marches, whilst a physical training instructor, assisted by
O'Grady, took charge of the " jerks." For the afternoons
a series of contests was arranged between the sections, and
included cross-country running, tug-o'-war, football, hand-
ball, and boxing. Points were allotted, and the section with
the highest aggregate, the signallers, secured the prize.
On the 21st two lorries being available, a party paid a visit
to Amiens. The fine cathedral, the shops, the boulevards
and the market were duly admired, but low tide in the
Battery exchequer had permitted an allowance of something less than two francs per man, so that no rash purchases
were made. Another party paid a visit to the same city
a few days later, and then rumours of a move became current.
These, however, were slightly premature, and the usual
routine continued.

The comic fire piquet was a feature which perhaps
should receive mention. The tour of duty was spent more
or less at the fire-station, opposite to which stood a convenient estaminet. The first rule on the list of duties
intimated that in case of fire a man should be sent to inform
the Town Major ; but nobody knew where the Town Major
lived, and, worse still, nobody could find out how the
" pompe " worked. Nevertheless the members of the piquet
trusted to luck, fortified themselves with eggs, chips, and
vin blanc, and prevented unseemly intrusion at night by
running the pump cart against the double doors on the inside.

Our pleasant stay at this village came to an end on
Sunday, January 27th, when we packed up once more and
left for Doullens. From here we went north to Arras,
and without stopping on the way returned to Etricourt
and unloaded the guns, while high overhead a Boche plane

attacked by anti-aircraft batteries shone like a silver fly in the beam of the searchlights. Accommodation for the night was found under canvas not far from the station. Clear and frosty weather prevailed, and the next day, after considerable waiting about, the guns moved off about 5.30 p.m. by road, while the remaining men went by Decauville from the station. Many of us can recall clearly that night. A full moon was rising, and the trees alongside the track seemed to form in places an avenue through which we passed. Very little could be recognised as we scanned the country from the open trucks, but soon the ruined walls of Fins were passed, and now, drawn by a motor engine, we skirted Dessart Wood and came on to the higher ground which overlooked the front. It was on this Gouzeaucourt sector that the enemy had, on November 30th, made a surprise thrust and taken Gonnelieu, but at this period things were fairly quiet again, and we settled down in the convenient sunken road, taking over from 51 Siege, whose turn to go on rest had come round. Plentiful supplies of wood and water were obtainable, and fine weather continued.

Within a few hours of arrival a curious discovery was made on the eastern side of the sunken road. On an improvised stretcher, beside a half-dug grave, lay a carefully finished, life-size effigy of a British soldier. Rumour at once flew round that any attempt to lift the stretcher would explode a mine laid so as to wreck the deep dug-out. But nothing occurred when the stretcher was taken for firewood, and the mystery of this effigy remained unsolved. Enemy activity caused us little concern in this position, but we were within pip-squeak range, and shells of this and heavier calibres were often fired on the dump 200 yards behind us, the camp near Fins, and the cross-roads at the northern end of the sunken road in which we lived. It was here that the wounding of Gunner Gomm, our only casualty in this position, took place. Almost every night heavily laden Gothas passed overhead and proceeded to bomb Fins, but the Christmas pantomime there continued its run, playing always to full houses. Very little firing was done by the Battery, and more than once officers and men with nothing to do on a fine afternoon turned out with the Battery dog for a couple of hours' ratting.

Our two O.P.'s on this sector were " Northern," situated about an hour's walk from the Battery, and " Bubble." At the latter occurred an interesting episode. Our officer on duty there was engaged, according to instructions, in carrying out liaison duty with some South African machine gunners manning a trench just in front. As is well known, the fatiguing nature of these duties necessitates a certain period for rest and refreshment, and the officer found his hosts exceedingly keen on hearing particulars of the 6-inch howitzer. He had hardly warmed to his subject when a telephonist informed him that conditions were favourable, and that the Battery, not having fired before, was about to test the correctness of the line. The officer at once invited his hearers to watch the shoot, but they were not shown the exact position of the target, which happened to be a cross-roads, and when the first shot fell about half a mile to the right of it, and flames and smoke shot up into the air, he turned blandly to the awestruck South Africans, saying, " There you are—I've put up a dump first shot," and laid in their minds the foundations of a lifelong respect for the Garrison Artillery. Needless to say the line was corrected, and the Mess enjoyed the story over the dessert. Our stay came to an end on February 27th, when we handed over to the relieving battery and took to the road once more.

HERMIES

The right section of the Battery left Gouzeaucourt for Hermies on the night of the 26th February, 1918, a bright moonlight night, with the inevitable Gothas overhead. The left section followed on the night of the 27th. The four guns were placed in their original positions near the railway bank, and the morning of the 28th found the Battery ready for action. Our former dug-outs in Havrincourt Wood, which we had occupied during December, 1917, were not available, and a miscellaneous collection of well-ventilated iron huts was commandeered to shelter officers and men. Atmospheric conditions were very severe, and spells of hard frost and snowstorms turned our ramshackle billets into refrigerators.

To prevent enemy airmen from photographing movement in and around the Battery position men were kept away from the guns except during action, and the minimum of work was done while snow lay on the ground. Leave being plentiful, each day would see two or three trim, polished gunners bidding farewell to their chums, and starting for the leave train at Bapaume. Life in Hermies during the early days of March consisted of " stand to " from 5 a.m. to 6.30 a.m.; Battery parade at 9.30 a.m.; and reliefs for digging deep dug-outs, under supervision of Australian tunnellers.

An unfortunate incident occurred about 9.15 a.m. on the 8th March, which robbed the Battery of two splendid gunners, and No. 4 Sub of two fine chums. Gunner H. Jeffries and Gunner G. L. Wolfe were working with an Australian sapper at the entrance of a deep dug-out when a stray Boche shell hit the entrance and killed the three men instantaneously. All the officers and men that could be spared from the Battery attended the funeral of our two comrades, who were buried in the British cemetery at Hermies, near " Windy Corner."

Although observation gave slight evidence of enemy activity, yet the higher command were aware that preparations were being made for an attack on this part of the front ; and during the days of apparent inertia within the Boche lines British artillery defence schemes were put into operation, and barbed wire was placed in front of all reserve trenches around the Battery. Squadrons of Gothas occasionally bombed the vicinity of Havrincourt Wood in daylight, the enemy artillery aeroplanes also being active. Throughout this period of preparation all ranks were confident in the belief that the Boche offensive would be broken by the artillery on the front.

On the night of 11th March, Hermies was heavily bombarded with gas shells, and Signaller James Duncan, who was making his way from one dug-out to another, was badly wounded. His cry for help attracted the attention of Q.M.S. C. Burch and Sergt. James Black, who dashed into the shellfire and brought the wounded man under cover. Signaller Duncan was badly wounded in both legs and his right arm partially blown off. But for the medical knowledge of his rescuers it is a question whether he could have survived.

The following night, 12th March, S.O.S. was signalled by coloured rockets from the trenches, and all guns on the front opened in reply. We had intervals of gunfire until dawn the next morning, which prevented the enemy attack from developing. Owing to the heavy casualties suffered by 68 S.B., R.G.A., during the enemy gas bombardment, 20 men and two N.C.O.'s were despatched from our Battery to enable 68 S.B. to carry on.

Hermies on the night of the 20th March was as peaceful as any English hamlet. In front a " B.E." hovered over the trenches, taking a final look at the Boche rear areas before returning to its aerodrome. In the gathering dusk traffic appeared on the various roads carrying rations and ammunition to the men in the line. The gunners stood in groups near the guns talking of " Blighty," ready for action when needed. Later the ruins of the village were enfolded by the cloak of night, and the moon, shining high in the heavens, cast weird shadows on the white road. The sentry, keeping a sharp look out, paced beside the guns.

An hour before dawn on the 21st March enemy trench mortar activity denoted " something doing," and the Battery received orders to stand by the guns. Soon the trench mortar bombardment was superseded by a gun barrage which swept our trenches and rear areas. Coloured rockets burst in the sky, the S.O.S. signal from our infantry. Almost simultaneously the British guns boomed out their deep growl of defiance, and in a moment the neighbourhood was turned into a roaring inferno.

Owing to the gas and dense fog it was with difficulty the layers managed to lay their guns. Piquet lamps were just visible, and to do gunfire with gas respirators fixed to the face was no easy task, but thanks to previous gas drill this Boche scheme to silence our artillery was frustrated. At 5.45 a.m. a shell landed in No. 3 gun-pit, smashing the trail of the gun and killing Gunner W. Armstrong. Immediately after the explosion Corporal B. Mundell, in charge of the gun, removed his gas mask and endeavoured to render first aid to the unfortunate man, but death had been instantaneous. Gunner W. Armstrong and his brother, Gunner F. Armstrong, had been associated with the Battery from the early days at King's Park, Edinburgh, and the officers and men deeply regretted the death of one of its original members.

So heavily did the Boche bombard the locality that it seemed as if every enemy gun was trained on our Battery position. A wounded gunner—J. S. Hannan—emerged from the smoke pervading No. 2 gun-pit, reporting the death of Gunner A. Mitchell and Gunner E. H. Rawlings, and the wounding in action of Corporal H. McNaughton and Gunner J. S. Oxley. The Battery will always remember the happy and generous character of Gunner A. Mitchell (" Pingy "), and the kindly and cheerful manner of Gunner E. H. Rawlings. All through the morning the gunners kept the two remaining guns in action, under murderous shellfire, until the Battery Commander gave the order " take cover." Later, a request was made for a volunteer gun crew, and Sergt. J. Johnston, Corporal B. Mundell, Corporal A. Garven, and Signaller W. Fraser responded to the call. During all the barrage Sergt. James Black carried out his arduous duties with a fearlessness which commanded the respect of all ranks.

Morning merged into forenoon without any appreciable abatement of the Boche bombardment. Time after time the guns were manned, but after short spells of " gunfire " the men were forced to seek shelter. Officers and men appreciated the pitiful plight of the gallant infantry in front, and every man gave of his best. Early in the afternoon No. 4 gun was again put in action, and with 2nd Lieut. A. K. Smith as a gun number, kept up a steady rate of fire. The gunners were feeling tired and hungry, and one by one they crawled out of the gun-pit to snatch a few moments' rest. As each one departed another man filled his place. After a perilous journey through Havrincourt Wood, the 22 men who had been attached to 68 S.B. returned about 3 p.m. to the Battery.

In the early evening D. B. Ross was wounded, and this popular and good-humoured Bombardier was carried to a dressing station by a stretcher party. The enemy shelling again reached a point of intensity, but our one gun remained in action. Communication between the guns and the Battery Commander's Post, which had been transferred to the deep dug-out under the railway bank, was severed, and Signalling Lance-Bombardier James Parker undertook to lay out a new line. He was mortally wounded as he neared the completion of his task, and died on the way to the dressing station. Bombardier Parker acted courageously all day, assisted by a small but brave group of signallers.

An order was issued about 6 p.m. to withdraw by sections to our rear position at Neuville, but Headquarters could not guarantee the arrival of motor lorries owing to the condition of the shell-torn roads. Meanwhile the military situation around Hermies became hourly more serious, the enemy advancing on both flanks and threatening our communications. Lieut. C. Jackson, M.C., and Artificer Staff-Sergeant G. Brown superintended all preparations for the destruction of the guns in the event of the position having to be abandoned. But as the result of unofficial information regarding the position in front of Hermies, which was being stubbornly defended by the 17th Division, a middle course was adopted after a short conference had been held in the B.C. Post. At 2.30 a.m., March 22nd, the personnel of the Battery, taking with them breech blocks and dial sights, withdrew to Neuville.

The Battery paraded at 9 a.m. the same morning before

Lieut.-Colonel Holdsworth-Hunt, D.S.O., who commended the officers and men on their good work during the opening stages of the enemy offensive, and about 9.30 a.m. a party of 50 men, under the command of Captain G. H. Cooke, M.C., started for Hermies to withdraw the guns. The journey to the Battery position will be remembered by all who took part in it. There was scarcely a portion of ground which did not receive attention from enemy guns. Shrapnel and high explosive burst to the right and left of the party, but Captain Cooke piloted the men to Hermies without a single mishap. Our guns stood as we had left them. Without delay, and under direct enemy observation, the gunners commenced to man-handle the four howitzers to the road near the position. Enemy aeroplanes hovered 1,000 feet above the scene, but all ranks maintained a cheerful *sang-froid*. By noon all guns had been removed from the gas-infested gun-pits, and placed in readiness for the arrival of the F.W.D.'s. After a short rest the party endeavoured to pull the guns to a 60-pounder bridge over the Canal du Nord, but two enemy aeroplanes with well-directed machine gun fire forced the men to seek cover in No. 4 Sub dug-out. A wireless message regarding the location of our guns must have been communicated to the Boche heavy artillery, as almost immediately 5·9's burst with alarming rapidity around the railway bridge. For nearly two hours the neighbourhood was heavily shelled, and every moment we expected a hit on the rickety dug-out, but the gods were kind, and somewhere about 2.15 p.m. the Boche emptied guns with a screeching salvo. Under intermittent machine-gun fire stores and kits were collected and all confidential maps and papers destroyed. Lieuts. Christie and Pinder arrived late in the afternoon bringing the news that motor lorries were on their way to evacuate guns, stores, and men. The clear moonlight night facilitated the complete withdrawal of the Battery without further casualties, and about 10 p.m. the F.W.D.'s started for Neuville carrying guns and gunners to safety.

E

THE RETREAT

A small party of men were at Neuville preparing a battery position on the afternoon of March 22nd when telephone communication was re-established with Hermies, and the work was hurried on and finished by 6 p.m. in readiness for the guns. Lorries arrived with 400 rounds of ammunition, which was quickly unloaded, but an hour later it was all loaded again, as instructions had been given that the guns were not to pull in at Neuville, but to proceed to Rocquigny. The Neuville party therefore set out for this place about midnight. The moon was almost full, and a considerable amount of traffic was passed on the way. Véry lights were going up in unexpected places, and ammunition dumps were blazing and exploding as the lorries passed. On arriving at Rocquigny we found three guns ready to be pulled into position, but the fourth had gone by mistake for a trip round Bapaume, and arrived at 5 a.m. All was ready for action at 6 a.m., and the Battery proceeded to breakfast, the first decent meal since the 20th. Then we got a few hours' sleep in the huts near by, and during the day did occasional firing, but owing to lack of information about the position of the British front line our activity was limited. The Boche guns were now moving forward, and during the afternoon some 5·9's pitched round the huts, and at tea-time an 8-inch gun was within range, making things very uncomfortable. From midday onwards we watched Infantry and Field Artillery retiring down the road, and wondered uneasily what chance we should have of getting away, but we found a few days later that these troops had been relieved by others, and that our inferences had been mistaken.

At 7 p.m. Brigade sent orders that we were to withdraw to a position near Combles. In bright moonlight the guns were pulled out, but the roads were so crowded with transport that it was impossible to get away, and not until 11 p.m. were we able to move off along the Le Transloy road. Near Sailly-Saillisel information was received that the Boche was in Combles, so the lorries made for Albert, which was reached about 3 a.m. on the morning of the 24th. We must have had a close shave, as a 60-pounder battery and a field battery which we passed near Sailly-Saillisel were both captured. From now onwards reassuring rumours began to spring up like mushrooms, a favourite story being that of the fall of Ostend.

After a few hours' sleep in the shattered houses of Albert we had breakfast, and then explored the town, which had not yet been evacuated by the inhabitants. Here a great number of field post-cards were despatched to reassure the anxious folks at home, and it is doubtful whether the postal authorities noticed that the name of every man in the Battery, for that day at least, was *Albert*. At 1 p.m. the Battery limbered up and took the road for Contalmaison, passing on the way scores of Chinese making tracks for safety. The " Chinks " were carrying their belongings in the usual quaint style, huge bundles being slung on the ends of a bamboo resting on the shoulder, while in some cases a record speed was being attained with loaded wheelbarrows. The guns were placed in a small valley to the south of Contalmaison, and here we found a large number of the retiring troops taking a short rest, but they were soon. compelled to move off again, as four Boche planes began to bomb and machine-gun them. Late in the evening a horseman was seen galloping up the moonlit road chased overhead by an enemy plane from which machine-gun bullets whizzed down. The rider fortunately caught sight of the lorries and turned into the shadow beside them, wishing, by the look of him, that his horse were small enough to come underneath with the rest of us.

On the ridge behind the Battery a visual station was established for communication with Brigade. This was manned up to midnight, when the party was recalled to lay a line to 68 Siege Battery on the Bapaume road. Our main task of firing took place from 2 a.m. to 6.30 a.m., and while this was in progress an attempt was made to find out the state of affairs in front, and Sergt. Black and Bombardier Leach went out to do so. They were, however, unsuccessful, and returned in the morning. The relief off duty found quarters for the night in a deserted " Chink " camp to the right front of the Battery, and came back in the morning with various souvenirs which our Eastern brethren had in their haste left behind. Just after breakfast on the 25th an officer from one of the Infantry Brigades came into the B.C. Post and asked whether the Battery would open fire on a wood about 4,000 yards away. The target was immediately engaged, but not more than thirty rounds had been fired when orders were received to pull out at once, as the enemy were advancing up the ridge in front. No one seemed anxious to make acquaintance with a German prisoners-of-war cage, so everything was loaded up and the position was cleared in the record time of eight minutes.

Back the lorries went to Albert, which was now a scene of confusion. Civilians were making a wild attempt to save their belongings, hurriedly packing carts and barrows with valuables and necessaries, and leaving the town by the western exits. Enemy planes had bombed the place heavily on the previous night, and among the ruins lay dead cats, dogs, and horses. Down one street came the manager of the Y.M.C.A. trundling his personal effects on a wheelbarrow, down another came groups of civilians heavily laden with awkward bundles. When the guns were placed in position near the prisoners-of-war cage on the outskirts of the town, a party of signallers was sent out to gather telephone cable, and while some men went to the cage and proceeded to make up their deficiencies of kit, others went to have a look round the streets of Albert once more. The E.F.C. and Y.M.C.A., well stocked as usual, had been abandoned, as there was no hope of obtaining transport to save the goods. It was obviously the duty of any British subject to prevent such property falling into the possession of the enemy, and chocolate, biscuits and tinned fruit, as well as cigarettes and champagne, were saved from the grasp of alien hands. This gallantry was not officially recognised, but there is little doubt that the action brought its own reward, and we soon arrived at that climax of luxury which is indicated by the refusal of an offered " Boguslavsky."

Lieut. Christie, who had used an O.P. on Bouzincourt Ridge during the preliminary bombardment for the Somme offensive of 1916, now went to the same post with two signallers, while the Battery was ordered to go forward

again, this time to Fricourt ; but we had only been there
an hour when Colonel Houldsworth Hunt arrived and told
us to return to Albert, as although the situation was fairly
good, the General was not prepared to make a stand just
yet. We returned to a position near Albert, but at once
received orders to go to the eastern side of Millencourt.
Here, about 9 a.m. on the 26th, a few 4·2's fell near the
Battery, but during the day we were not much disturbed.
Enemy aircraft dropped a few bombs, and one of our observation planes was forced to descend close by, the pilot having
been killed.   In the afternoon enemy infantry advancing
over Poziéres Ridge was engaged, and from the O.P. at
Bouzincourt these troops were seen advancing in force down
the slope towards Albert.   At this point our position was
spotted by the enemy, who bombarded the Battery heavily
with 5·9's, so the guns were pulled out again and placed near
.a bank behind Millencourt, while shells continued to fall
on the spot just vacated.   Firing was now carried on con-
tinuously for about five hours, and at 9 p.m. we heard the
disquieting rumour that the Boche cavalry had broken
through.   This naturally caused some excitement, and the
despatch rider, Gunner H. Punton, was sent forward to pick
up news.   He returned with the information that the old
trenches just in front of Millencourt were being manned by
the infantry.   At the same time our men going to billets in
Henencourt were machine-gunned by a Boche plane, and
Gunner Cooper was wounded.   It was now decided to
withdraw to Warloy, but no sooner had the lines of fire
been laid out than orders were received to return once more
to Millencourt.   Billets were re-occupied in Henencourt,
and the night was fairly quiet, but after breakfast Millencourt, which was under enemy observation, was again
heavily bombarded, and orders were then given for a withdrawal to our previous position.   At this juncture the
Australians took over the line in front of us, and a period
of stationary warfare began.

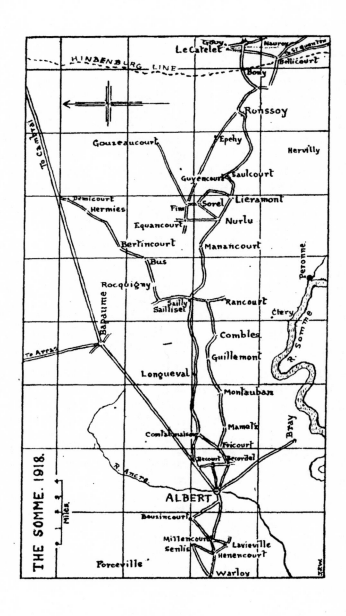

THE SOMME. 1918.

WARLOY

The close of the retreat found us in Warloy Baillon, a small village in the valley of the Hallue, to the west of Henencourt Ridge, which overlooks the Ancre valley. Here we spent the late spring and summer of 1918, enjoying phenomenally fine weather, and although within reach of enemy artillery, were seldom troubled by his long range weapons. Looking to the east from Warloy, Henencourt Wood can be seen on the ridge, and it was at the north-east corner of the wood that the Battery took up position on the 29th of March, when the vigour of the enemy advance had spent itself. No further retirement was to be made on our part, and the famous " backs to the wall " message from Sir Douglas Haig was published throughout the army.

· The Battery position was rather open to hostile observation, and when it was found that the enemy was ranged on us, and replied to every shot we fired, it was deemed advisable to take advantage of the cover afforded by the wood, behind which, on the right-hand side of the Warloy-Henencourt road, the guns were soon placed. The B.C. Post, which had been during the retreat installed in a lorry, was now transferred to a tent, and small shelters for the detachments were made behind the guns. To our left front was Aveluy Wood and village, with the high Somme country farther east. Directly in front, situated low in the valley, lay Albert, while farther right, also on the river, were Méaulte, Dernancourt, and Buiré. Well to the south of our sector was the scene of the thrust for Amiens, and day and night the heavy sound of firing could be heard from that direction, but except for occasional supporting fire on the flank of the Australian corps engaged there, our business lay with the country immediately in front. The enemy communications were harassed night after night ; Albert was made almost untenable, and every opportunity was taken of damaging those batteries which had ventured up too close.

· The village of Warloy, which from a distance looked rather idyllic with its trees and red-tiled roofs, had been untouched by the tide of war during the previous Somme campaign, but the buildings were rather unsubstantial structures of mud and sticks, and it was in a large barn of this type that the men of the Battery were—to misuse a term—housed. Fortunately ample supplies of water could be obtained from the well of the hot-tempered old lady across the road, and on fine days the *al fresco* bath under the apple trees behind the barn became very fashionable. Here also tasty suppers were prepared in the evenings consisting of fried potatoes, eggs, and pork, the latter being purchased at ruinous prices from that greyhaired old brigand the butcher, whose shop was at the eastern end of the village.

On the 5th of April the Boche renewed his attack and succeeded in getting a direct hit on the officers' mess in the village, wounding Gunner Mugleston ; while on the 9th mustard gas was sent over into the wood in front of the position, but to no purpose as far as the Battery was concerned. In fact, during all this period it was obvious that we held the upper hand in the matter of shelling. Whenever the enemy was suspected of an inclination to attack, elaborate schemes of counter-preparation were put into force, and suspected areas, roads, tracks and batteries were subjected to heavy fire. It was not because the enemy was unaware of our position that he refrained from answering in kind, since on his maps that we picked up when advancing, every position we occupied on this sector had been correctly marked. On the morning of the 16th of April an enemy aeroplane, flying low, appeared to be making observations on the Battery area, and in the afternoon between two and three o'clock the Australian horse lines situated about 500 yards to our rear were shelled. Many horses were killed, the remainder galloping frantically in all directions until caught and brought back by the horsemen. On this same afternoon the Madonna on the tower of Albert Cathedral was knocked down by shellfire, a well-established army legend disappearing at the same time.

On the 17th, as a precautionary measure, the two sections of the Battery were placed farther apart, the left section being moved about a mile away to a position on the Senlis road, with orders to fire on nothing but S.O.S. calls. Dugouts were made in the open, and camouflaging had to be extensively practised. On the night of the 20th enemy shelling of the road drove us out of the cook-house and B.C. Post tent, and a better position had to be found for these two important institutions. Once settled down, there was little to do at the left section at this time, as the unscreened position was under balloon observation, and little movement during the day was permissible. The road and eastern side of the valley were often shelled; the 6-inch battery on the outskirts of Senlis, and the 60-pounders near the corner of the wood, being the enemy's favourite targets. Round this corner ran our O.P. line, and many a lively half-hour the signallers had when mending the constant breaks which occurred.

On the 24th April there was a big attack at Villers-Brettonneux, and the right section turned out in response to an S.O.S. call at 4 a.m. The left section was shelled on the 10th of May, and on the 14th the Warloy balloon, which had worked in conjunction with the Battery, and floated just over the billets, was burnt by an enemy plane, which, however, did not succeed in returning to its own lines. About a week later we were especially active in counter-preparation, and there was a good deal of speculation as to coming events. Just at this time the German forces were at their greatest strength on the western front, and news from the south, where desperate fighting took place round Rheims towards the end of the month, was anxiously awaited. Night and morning visual stations were manned, but the occasion for their use in action never came. May was an uneventful month, except that on the 30th the right section was subjected to a fairly heavy dose of gas and high explosive, but fortunately no casualties occurred, and on the 5th of June the guns were removed to a new position in the dry bed of a stream not far from the left section. About this time Major Saunders having transferred to the R.F.C., Captain Cooke was promoted to Major in command of the Battery.

To an onlooker there was little indication in the peaceful village of Warloy and the Senlis valley of the critical state of our fortunes at this time. It is true that on Sunday morning, June the 2nd, some long range shelling, apparently intended for the balloon station, made our billets much too hot to hold us; and at a Church parade in the orchard on the following Sunday attention was instantly diverted from the hymn-books to the sky when a Boche plane, flying at a height of about 60 yards, passed overhead. A shell burst just behind the tail of the machine, but, without altering course, the aviator proceeded to our nearest aerodrome and gave himself up. At night the Gothas passed over to bomb the rear areas, and the long range guns shelled Contay or Baizieux, but for some reason or other Warloy received little of this unwelcome attention. It was, however, deemed advisable to remove artillery units from the village, and as a result of a Corps order we spent the 16th-23rd June preparing dug-outs in a chalk bank which overlooked the village from the south. This was a healthy and pleasant situation, and the walk to the Battery led through great stretches of green wheat gorgeous with poppies and cornflowers. On the 29th June the Battery was engaged in a wire-cutting shoot to the right of Albert, the object of which was to divert attention from the actual attack about to take place on the left. Reinforcing artillery suddenly pulled in near the B.C. Post in the Senlis valley, and on the 30th the attack was successfully carried out. While on this front we were well situated for observation, though at first the work was done under rather exposed conditions. Our first posts were situated in and near the Maze, a network of trenches forming a strong point reached by communication trenches, which were here and there crossed by tracks or roads. At every track or road the party going to or coming from O.P. had to leave the trench, and the enemy made the most of these opportunities for sniping. Conditions improved later, when an O.P., called Solo, had been made to the left front of Millencourt. A number of N.C.O.'s who had had no previous experience of observation work were here given an opportunity of spending a day at the front.

The post had to be manned at dawn, and on these fine summer mornings the officer, two signallers, and the observer would start with rations, telephone, and observation instruments in the direction of Henencourt. Passing through the wood they came to the chateau, a handsome building considerably damaged by one or two direct hits, but affording quarters for a considerable number of officers and men. They then followed the path through the garden, and emerged by a hole in the wall on to the open track to the communication trenches. Here a board announced that you were under observation as far as the next dip, but if, as usual, the morning mist still hung in the valley, the party did not take to the camouflaged road. Through the corn-fields and past the 18-pounders the track led to Wallaby Trench and Australia Street, and after a long series of twists and turns the observation post was reached. The clearest view was always obtained after midday, when the opposite slope of the Ancre valley stood out sharply. Radi-ating from Albert ran the Bapaume, Becourt, Becordel, and Bray roads, and these were under close observation as long as visibility lasted. On clear days the flags on the German Red Cross Hospital at Montauban, as well as the shunting trains on the Maricourt Plateau, could be plainly seen. At the foot of the slope, on the crest of which the O.P. was situated could be seen the front and second line of both British and German trenches. Between them was a wide No Man's Land covered with standing corn, and away to the left were the tall, ruined houses of Albert, overtopped by the cathedral tower. Other points which stood up prominently were the farm buildings between the front lines, the deserted huts in the old British prisoners-of-war cage, the straggly dead trees behind Albert known as Black Wood, Bellevue Farm, with its clock tower, and Shamrock Tree on the Becourt road. During the four months spent in watching this front these places became very familiar, and received continuous attention from the Battery, but it was only in the early morning and at dusk that much move-ment could be distinguished. Transport attempting to enter or leave Albert got a warm time *en route*, and for about three weeks in June the ration parties of the enemy coming through the cornfields every evening were per-sistently sniped and harassed. To members of the O.P. party who had been forced many a time to skip it along the countryside because of Fritz's dirty work with 4·2's and 5·9's, it gave great satisfaction when he was seen bolting and ducking in his turn. The effectiveness of the shooting was proved by prisoners' statements published soon after-wards in Corps Intelligence. The night O.P. during this period was Poker, a square stone building situated at the corner of Henencourt Chateau garden. It was furnished with Louis Quatorze armchairs, a good stove, and a comfortable wire bed. A look-out slot was made by knocking out a large corner stone, and under these conditions it was possible to await morning and the relieving party with a more or less philosophical mind.

On July 2nd we left the Senlis position to relieve 225 S.B. at Millencourt, where from a position about 3,000 yards from the line counter-battery work was being carried out. Shortly after our arrival the S.O.S. went up four times, and in the Boche attack that night the ground gained on the 30th of June was lost again. With aeroplane and neutralising shoots the enemy batteries were given little rest, and on the whole we received little in the way of a systematic reply, two men only, Gunner Burnett and Gunner Kenna, being slightly wounded during our stay there. In fact, the worst attack was delivered by quite another enemy. Spanish influenza began to make headway, and the deep dug-out was suspected of being the source of infection. At any rate, by the 7th of July 57 men were ill, and it became necessary to hand over the right section guns to 68 S.B. Counter-battery work was continued ; day after day a Boche battery would be reported to Brigade as firing on some point in our lines, and from Brigade would come the order to put, say, 50 rounds on XY 35, XY 12, or XY 9. At any hour of the day or night such an order might be expected, and aeroplane photographs of these battery positions showed how effective the shooting had been.

Meanwhile parties of our convalescent men were being sent down to Le Treport, a pleasant little coast town northeast of Dieppe. Here the complete change, the healthy camp on high ground, the food, and perhaps the mixed bathing brought about a speedy return of health and spirits. On the 18th of July occurred an event which indirectly concerned us very much. Marshal Foch, as he himself has said, being unable to defend any longer on the Marne, decided to attack, and this was the turn of the tide. Warloy now became a target, and on the nights of the 6th and 9th of August heavy bombs were dropped there, two within 50 yards of the billets and another among the houses. A high-velocity gun also shelled the roads and tracks on the southern side of the village. On August 8th the Fourth Army attacked on our right, and, advancing eastwards from the lines in front of Amiens, captured 20,000 prisoners and many guns. Successes like this soon began to affect our sector, and attention was aroused by the fact that the Boche blew up what remained of the tower of Albert Cathedral, and cut down that prominent feature of the landscape known as Pear Tree. On the 18th August a local operation to seize jumping-off ground took place on our right, and at this time the front began to lose its stationary character as batteries moved forward and dumps and billets followed. On the 20th the Fifth Corps successfully attacked on our left, and on the 21st there was a small attack in front to secure more jumping-off ground. Albert was then attacked at 4.45 a.m. on the morning of the 22nd with success, though Black Wood and Bellevue Farm held up our men for a time. The whole front was now on the move, and our next position was almost due east to Bouzincourt on the 23rd, where, supporting an attack in front, we took part in a heavy barrage opening at 1 a.m. on the morning of the 24th. On the 25th the chase began in earnest, and, evacuating the billets in Warloy, the personnel, with guns, motor lorries, and stores, crossed the front line we had held since March, and commenced to follow up the retreating enemy.

THE ADVANCE

The Battery had learnt something about mobility in the retreat, and the knowledge was put to good use in the advance. When a halt was made only the necessary stores were unloaded ; the F.W.D.'s went forward pulling the guns into position, and the gunners went on duty carrying all their belongings. The motor transport was parked close at hand, ready as soon as the guns were pulled out to follow up with the men off duty to find fresh billets. At each position the Battery stayed as a rule for a few days only, yet ammunition, food, and the mail came up regularly the whole time. Sleeping accommodation was often found in dug-outs and huts abandoned only a few days before by the enemy, and as many of these places had been mined, a system of examination was instituted, and carried out by the Royal Engineers.

We now passed through Albert, which was completely ruined. Great masses of masonry had fallen into the streets, leaving barely enough room for the guns to pass. A bridge had just been completed by which we crossed the Ancre, and then turned south to a position on the Vivier Mill road. The cross-roads at this mill were in a fearful mess, the result of our nightly tasks of bombardment ; and visits paid by members of the Battery to gun positions near Méaulte and to Bellevue Farm, which was reduced to heaps of bricks, provided evidence of the effectiveness of the work done by our heavy artillery on this sector. We were already out of range on reaching this position on August 25th, so the next day we pulled out, passed through Albert again, and turned up the Becordel road, proceeding east by Becordel-Becourt on the right and Fricourt on the left to the next stopping place. The Battery position, so we were told, was in Mametz Church, but although there was some shelter for the detachments in the half-ruined crypt, the scene above ground was typical of the utter desolation of the Somme country. There was no sign of a church—simply uneven ground clothed in green turf ; and of the village there remained only a few fragments of brickwork, with here and

Major G. H. COOKE M.C.

there a stray garden plant. Our firing was directed on miscellaneous targets, and when after a barrage the infantry went over and could not get into touch with the enemy, we moved up on the 29th to Guillemont, taking up a position just where the road turns off to Combles. The detachments found temporary shelter in the high bank near the guns, and the B.C. Post was installed in one of the many huts in our old casualty clearing station there. The casualties among the enemy's horses at this spot had been heavy, and many of the huts had been badly damaged. In the afternoon a large squadron of enemy planes flew over the district, and doubtless the constant stream of traffic at this busy corner was observed, with the result that some hot shelling took place all round the Battery and among the huts. During the night the enemy fired with heavier calibres on the same target, and a shell pitching within two yards of the doorway, upset the hut from which the B.C. Post had been removed to a dug-out just after teatime that evening. In the huts round about were found many of the wooden beds which Fritz made in abundance, as well as the sandbags of paper cloth, which reminded us of both German shortage and German ingenuity. Men were forbidden to pick the flowers, so the German notice on one of the huts informed us, but the gardens contained only dead horses, and these it was advisable to pass on the windward side.

On August 30th the billets moved up to Montauban, and with the help of a few tents and the deserted German huts there we found sufficient accommodation. This was historic ground, for away on the left were the gaunt dead trees of High Wood and Delville Wood, round which the terrible fighting of 1916 took place. In the early morning of September 2nd the guns moved up to Combles, where ample room was found in sheds, cellars, and dug-outs for the whole Battery. At this position the guns were not fired, and the enemy seemed to be evacuating with greater speed, though the outskirts of the village were shelled with shrapnel and heavy H.E. during our stay. The most striking sight in Combles was the traffic going up the line to supply our advancing army. Hour after hour troops, horses, wagons, and lorries streamed past without a pause, taking up reliefs, food, water, and ammunition.

The guns went forward again on the 3rd of September, and were placed on open ground by the side of the Bapaume-Peronne road, the surrounding country being mournful in the extreme, with its groups of wooden crosses and its thousands of grass-grown shell-holes. To the left was Sailly-Saillisel and to the right Rancourt, while straight ahead was St. Pierre Vaast Wood. We completed a short programme of firing here, watched the usual strings of prisoners filing past, and then, packing up ammunition and stores once more, went forward to Manancourt on the evening of the 5th, within 400 yards of the Boche. This village was under heavy fire, and signallers who went forward with cable had a warm time there. Under the trees in a large park some Boche headquarters staff had been housed, and a plentiful supply of maps had been left behind. Since at this place there was a practicable bridge which provided the only canal crossing in the district, both now and for days afterwards the long range guns which faced us during the whole advance shelled the approaches, and to be held up there was an uncomfortable experience. Again the guns did only a short spell of firing, and when the off duty party moved up, the Battery had already gone forward to Equancourt, on the night of the 6th, and to that place the lorries proceeded. This village, just west of Fins, was situated in pleasant country, over which there had been little fighting, and on its eastern edge was a wood through which came the sound of the continual enemy bombardment of Fins.

We were now as far east as we had been in the previous March, and were reminded of the fact by the roadside notice in the village giving the direction to Neuville. Hermies was unfortunately too near the line at this time to make a visit there advisable. On the night of the 7th September, after a stay of only one day at Equancourt, the guns moved forward again, while the fairly comfortable billets in that village were retained. Our position was situated near Sorel-le-Grand, and to reach it we had to pass through Fins. This place was being bombarded as usual, but having reached the southern outskirts safely, we were feeling somewhat relieved when suddenly the lorries ran straight into a gas shell bombardment which was being put over by the enemy field guns. Orders to leave the lorries were given, but in the darkness it was difficult to judge which direction was the best to take. Some men found shelter in trenches on the south side of the road, others ran among the old huts on the north side, and then following the Major, went up the wind to escape the gas. Crossing the open space on the north side of the huts, this party went through what it is hardly an exaggeration to call a shower of shells falling all round with their peculiar sputtering burst. Yet when a roll was called later in the night, it was found that not a man had been injured in any way, and the subsequent dropping of parachute lights and bombs in the vicinity caused little concern. It was evident that we were again close on the enemy's heels, and felt none too pleased when in the early morning, as all the battery was busily engaged in unpacking stores and pulling in the guns, a low-flying Boche plane came over and took stock of the whole proceeding. Little firing was done in this position, and for a time the enemy gave no intimation that we had been located. The ridge in front and the roadway on our left were shelled, but the men were now given a few days' rest in the billets at Equancourt while the position was occupied by a guard which had a few lively hours when the evening " strafes " began. At night there was plenty of aerial activity, and it was not unusual to be roused by the sound of cheers in the street, and to rush out to watch a Boche machine tumbling down in flames. Three came down in one night, and enemy raiding must have received a severe set-back.

On the afternoon of September 12th, having ranged his guns by aeroplane, the enemy proceeded to bombard the Battery position. Orders to move forward had been received, and F.W.D.'s and men arrived to pull out the guns on that evening. At first it was only possible to work during the longer intervals between the groups of rounds, and it was fortunate that most of the shots fell slightly plus of the position. After nightfall the firing ceased, and the Battery, after the usual difficulties on the soft, muddy ground, pulled out and moved off.

Two adjoining villages, Guyencourt and Saulcourt, are situated three miles to the south-east of Fins, and a small

F

valley runs westward from them down to Lieramont. On the rough, bushy ground near the two villages the guns were placed on the morning of September 13th, and the detachments began to make small shelters in the trenches round about. A cellar in Guyencourt served as a B.C. Post, and the cook-house and the wireless station were halfway between this and the guns. The high ridge about two and a half miles in front of us was held by those stubborn fighters, the Jaegers, the village of Epehy being strongly defended by machine-gun posts. Away on our left front was Cambrai, on our right front St. Quentin, and about seven miles due east was the Hindenburg line. A number of batteries occupied positions in the valley, and enemy fire at night was mainly of the searching and sweeping variety. On the morning of September 16th, during our preliminary bombardment of various targets, the enemy replied with a heavy fire which drove the men to take cover. After a lull they were called out for action once more, but from one of the dug-outs in which Bombardier Cull, Gunner S. W. Large, and Gunner Norminton had taken shelter there came no response. A shell had struck the dug-out and the unfortunate men were killed instantly. On the following morning the funeral, attended by officers and men of the Battery, took place at Nurlu Cemetery. Gunner Large had been with the Battery since Ypres, and Bombardier Cull and Gunner Norminton had joined us at Warloy. All three were men of that kindly and frank-natured type which the Battery could ill afford to lose.

On the night of the 17th more gas and high explosive was fired on the Battery, and men began to suffer from the usual inflammation of the eyes and loss of voice, but at 5.20 a.m. we took part in the bombardment, supporting another successful morning attack. During the day the gas, with which the ground had been soaked, began to rise, owing to the warmth of the sunshine, and finally about 30 N.C.O.'s and men, in addition to Lieut. James, were sent to hospital for treatment, while others remained under the doctor's supervision in the Battery. On September 25th the billets were moved from Equancourt to Guyencourt, where accommodation was found in a sunken road.

By this time the nightly bombardment of the position and the shelling round the B.C. Post, which was at first under observation, had ceased, but to the north-east the sky, lit up by gun-flashes and fires in the abandoned villages, reminded us of the fight going on round Cambrai. On September 26th the guns were pulled out and went forward to a position on the right of Epehy. Here we were once more within range, and the enemy bombarded heavily the ground behind the railway bank where we were. A couple of days were spent in battering the Hindenburg line, of which our Infantry were now almost within striking distance, and on Saturday evening, September 28th, we advanced to a valley in front of Ronssoy, just about a thousand yards from the enemy, whose machine gunners, hidden somewhere in the vicinity, swept the valley as the guns were being placed in position. The usual night firing was directed on this area where so much artillery was situated, and there was no encouragement to loiter when crossing from the road to the Battery. The B.C. Post was placed in a deep dug-out in the ragged-looking sunken road near by, and as the dug-out was shared by three batteries, the state of the gangways, stairs, and recesses when packed with sleeping men was the last word in overcrowding. On the 1st October a sad accident occurred. James Cryer, who had been in charge of the wireless station since September, 1917, was walking along the bank above the sunken road when a bomb, accidentally kicked by a passer-by, exploded and wounded him in the chest. Australians standing near immediately rendered first aid, and the wounded man was quickly removed to hospital. A more conscientious worker or good-natured comrade was not to be found in the Battery, and with great regret we heard later that this promising young fellow was no more.

On the ridge just in front of us were the tanks which had been knocked out a day or two previously, and only about a couple of miles away was the three-mile tunnel through which the St. Quentin Canal goes underground from Le Catelet to Bellicourt. Heavy concentrations were fired on all strong positions in the enemy lines, and on Sunday, September 29th, the news came through that Le Catelet had been taken, and that consequently the great line had been breached. American troops fighting there had, however, suffered severely, and little further progress had been made. The result was that when the Battery crossed the Hindenburg line at Bony on October 4th, and took up position on the western side of Railway Ridge, the guns had to be switched sixty degrees left of their original line to fire on Prospect Hill. The B.C. Post was here placed in a dug-out which had been a lamp signalling station, and also served as an O.P. for our firing on Beaurevoir. From this point we could scan the country for miles to the east, and see the church spires in villages which had not been destroyed. Ramicourt, Montbrehain, and Brancourt stood out clearly in the afternoon sunshine, and here and there in the fine stretches of rolling country stood the comfortable-looking farmsteads surrounded by clumps of trees.

We had not been long in this position when down the road came British lorries laden with old men, women, and children wildly excited at being once more free and among friends. From now onwards, having shifted the enemy from his fixed line of defence, our army adopted as far as possible the practice of outflanking villages, and taking them without direct artillery fire. On Sunday, October 6th, the guns once more moved, this time a mile and a half to the north-east, where in a small valley near Gouy we prepared for action. In laying the line to this position Signalling Sergeant G. Graves was wounded in the hand and head by a shell which burst near the party engaged in making a pole-crossing.

On the 7th the billets, which for a short time had been fixed at the inadequate sunken road position in front of Ronssoy, were moved up, and we soon began to explore the Catelet-Nauroy portion of the Hindenburg line with a view to finding apartments. Here were the stairways, wide enough for three men abreast to walk down without stooping. Forty steps down were the rooms complete with wooden walls, ceiling, and floor, glazed doors with porcelain handles, electric light connections, and a special pumping apparatus for changing the air. Here, too, were plank beds, forms, and tables, as well as stoves fitted with pipes reaching right up the stairway. All this desirable residence was

" To let,'' rent free, the owner having left to go abroad. Above ground there was little to be seen, although this line was still in course of extension at the time of its capture. Near by was the commencement of a shaft, with the windlass and the pair of little trucks which ran down the wooden railway to the man excavating below ; but one of our shells had smashed up the apparatus, and further excavation, owing to unforeseen circumstances, had to be abandoned. Other work was also left unfinished, including dozens of deep dug-outs which had only been worked on for a few days, and covered communication trenches in which men could move up to the line hidden from view by earth-covered stout wire netting. All round Gouy, the village near which the guns were situated, there was evidence of the heavy bombardment which had accompanied the taking of that place and Le Catelet, and again during the nights of the 6th and 7th October heavy gas shell was falling among the ruins.

An attack was to be made by us on the morning of October 8th. The Infantry forming-up line ran through Beaurevoir, and it was intended to advance about five or six thousand yards to a village called Serain. On our left the 5th Corps was to take Villers-Outreaux by an encircling movement, while on our right the Americans were to advance towards Fresnoy. About 1 a.m. a lively barrage was started by the Field Artillery in order to drown the noise of the tanks advancing into position, and about dawn the heavy artillery opened out on special targets, while the field artillery went through the lifting barrage programme once more. By breakfast-time we had completed our task, and though then unaware of the fact, had fired our last shell. Prisoners began to straggle down the road quite early, and the neighbouring 4·5 howitzers limbered up and went forward. Targets then began to come in by wireless, but our Infantry were advancing so quickly that it was not safe to open fire. Observation planes sent down map co-ordinates indicating the position of our advancing troops ; Serain was taken ; the cavalry went through, and the battle passed out of touch.

The shortening of the line consequent upon the rapid advance gave us an artillery strength per 1,000 yards of front much above the normal, and 89th Brigade, which had been composed of the same group of batteries since December, 1917, received instructions to pull out of the line and take a few days' rest. For four days we remained at the billets speculating as to the next move. All sorts of wild guesses were made, and one group of men divided the front into sectors and organised a sweepstake with reference to the next front on which we should go into action. By now, even the ration dumps had got in front of us, so it was high time to make a move, and we set out on our travels once more on the morning of October 12th.

AMMUNITION REPORT

Four original guns fired 56,281 rounds. Total ammunition expended in two years, 108,271 rounds, a weight of 4,833 tons, or, including cartridge, 5,000 tons. Nineteen guns in all have been used in 42 battery positions.

HONOURS AND AWARDS

Major G. H. COOKE, Military Cross (Demicourt).
Captain C. JACKSON, Military Cross (Arras).
Sergeant-Major M. O'HARA, Meritorious Service Medal.
Sergeant H. HAYES, Military Medal (Arras).
Sergeant J. BLACK, Military Medal (Hermies).
Sergeant J. JOHNSTON, Military Medal (Hermies).
Sergeant A. GARVEN, Belgian Croix-de-Guerre (Ypres).
Sergeant B. MUNDELL, French Croix-de-Guerre (Hermies).
Bombardier E. HAINES, Military Medal (Arras).
Gunner J. ARNOLD, Military Medal (Arras).
Gunner J. MUIR, Military Medal (Ypres).
Signaller E. C. WALTER, Belgian Croix-de-Guerre (Ypres).
Signaller O. KIERNAN, Meritorious Service Medal.

MENTIONED IN DISPATCHES

Major J. J. SAUNDERS (Arras and Ypres).
Major G. H. COOKE (Somme, 1918).
Signaller W. A. FRASER (Hermies).

APPOINTMENTS AND PROMOTIONS

OFFICERS.

Major J. J. SAUNDERS, to Kite Balloon Section, R.A.F.
Captain O. P. NIMMO, to 49 Siege Battery, R.G.A.
Captain C. JACKSON, to 278 Siege Battery, R.G.A.
Lieut. J. R. JAMIESON, to Fourth Army Calibration School.
Captain F. S. WEIR, to 3 Siege Battery, R.G.A.
Lieut. W. CHRISTIE, to 89th Brigade, R.G.A.

WARRANT OFFICERS, N.C.O.'s, AND MEN.

B.Q.M.S. A. J. CREIGHTON, to B.S.M. 64 Siege Battery, R.G.A.
B.Q.M.S. C. C. BURCH, to B.S.M. 57 Siege Battery, R.G.A.
B.Q.M.S. W. R. FIDOE, to 180 Siege Battery, R.G.A.
Staff-Sergt. F. HOLDEN, to 224 Siege Battery, R.G.A.
Corporal T. LAWRIE, to 444 Siege Battery, R.G.A.
Corporal R. GIBB, to Instructor, Home Establishment.
Corporal C. J. P. BREACH, to Instructor, Home Establishment.
Corporal J. HASTIE, to Instructor, Home Establishment.
Corporal R. NEISH, to Cadet School.
Corporal R. H. DAY, to Cadet School.
Bombardier J. J. CHAPPEL, to Cadet School.
Signaller O. KIERNAN, to Cadet School.

CASUALTIES

KILLED.	DATE.	PLACE OF BURIAL.
Gr. J. F. HARVEY	... 11/12/16	... Dainville (Arras).
Bdr. W. B. GILMOUR	... 25/5/17	... Tilloy (Arras).
Fitter G. H. MAYES	... 25/5/17	... Tilloy (Arras).
Gr. P. BONFIELD	... 25/5/17	... Tilloy (Arras).
Gr. W. B. HENDERSON	... 18/7/17	... Vlamertinghe (Ypres).
Gr. W. MOFFATT	... 27/7/17	... Vlamertinghe (Ypres).
Cpl. J. BRAIDWOOD	... 10/9/17	... St. Jean (Ypres).
Gr. H. JEFFRIES	... 8/3/18	... Hermies (Cambrai Sec.).
Gr. G. L. WOLFE	... 8/3/18	... Hermies (Cambrai Sec.).
Gr. W. H. ARMSTRONG	... 21/3/18	... Hermies (Cambrai Sec.).
Gr. A. MITCHELL	... 21/3/18	... Hermies (Cambrai Sec.).
Bdr. J. PARKER	... 21/3/18	... Hermies (Cambrai Sec.).
Gr. E. H. RAWLINGS	... 21/3/18	... Hermies (Cambrai Sec.).
Bdr. H. J. CULL	... 16/9/18	... Nurlu Cemetery (Le Catelet Sector).
Gr. S. W. LARGE	... 16/9/18	... Nurlu Cemetery (Le Catelet Sector).
Gr. W. NORMINTON	... 16/9/18	... Nurlu Cemetery (Le Catelet Sector).

DIED OF WOUNDS.	DATE.	PLACE OF BURIAL.
Bdr. J. DAVIS	... 29/4/17	... British Military Cemetery, Etaples, Grave No. 422.
Gr. A. J. S. TAIT	... 26/5/17	... British Military Cemetery, Agnez-des-Douissons.
Sgt. H. HAYES	... 7/7/17	... Soldiers' Cemetery, 3rd Canadian (Ypres Sector), C.C.S.
Gr. H. LAMBOURNE	... 6/12/17	
Gr. G. B. IRVING	... 10/12/17	
A.M. J. E. CRYER	... 6/10/18	

WOUNDED OR GASSED

OFFICERS.

2/Lt. D. K. WILSON	22/8/17
2/Lt. F. C. FOULSHAM	9/4/17
Major G. H. COOKE, M.C.	31/5/18
2/Lt. E. V. JAMES	18/9/18

N.C.O.'S AND MEN.

NAME.	DATE.	NAME.	DATE
Gr. J. R. ROBERTSON	20/3/17	Gr. A. COLEY... ...	12/9/17
Fitter W. SUNDERLAND	21/3/17	Gr. J. P. COOPER ...	12/9/17
Bdr. E. HAINES ...	23/4/17	Gr. D. CORMACK ...	12/9/17
Gr. H. PUNTON ...	2/5/17	Cpl. J. DAFFON ...	12/9/17
Gr. T. P. CRAIG ...	9/5/17	Gr. W. E. DOWNING	12/9/17
Gr. C. H. COLES ...	21/5/17	Gr. H. EMMETT ...	12/9/17
Gr. J. OSBORNE ...	2/7/17	Gr. D. T. EVANS ...	12/9/17
Gr. A. MOULD ...	3/7/17	Gr. A. H. HARDAKER	11/9/17
Gr. J. STILL	15/7/17	Gr. A. GARVEN ...	11/9/17
Gr. J. G. MUIR ...	18/7/17	Gr. S. KITCHEN ...	11/9/17
Bdr. J. McLEAN ...	18/7/17	Bdr. J. S. NIXON ...	11/9/17
Bdr. J. STRANG ...	18/7/17	Bdr. A. PAIRMAN ...	11/9/17
Bdr. T. M. CLARK ...	18/7/17	Gr. G. PALMER ...	11/9/17
Gr. P. LOMAS ...	27/7/17	Gr. T. S. RICHARDS ...	11/9/17
Bdr. A. PAIRMAN ...	9/8/17	Gr. A. ROWLES ...	11/9/17
Gr. D. JENKINS ...	20/8/17	Gr. S. SMITH	11/9/17
Gr. T. W. H. SHAW ...	25/8/17	Bdr. G. B. SHAW ...	11/9/17
Gr. D. JENKINS ...	14/5/17	Bdr. W. WARDELL ...	11/9/17
Gr. B. COCKER ...	25/8/17	Bdr. J. GLYNN ...	12/9/17
Gr. F. CRAWFORD ...	25/8/18	Bdr. A. LANE ...	12/9/17
Gr. T. WOOD... ...	26/8/17	Cpl. J. ANDERSON ...	12/9/17
Gr. H. BATES ...	30/8/17	Gr. FIDDLER... ...	12/9/17
Gr. T. GREEN ...	30/8/17	Gr. HOLME	12/9/17
Gr. J. F. SCOTT ...	2/9/17	Gr. D. WOOD... ...	12/9/17
Gr. A. LANE	2/9/17	Gr. T. PRESTON ...	12/9/17
Gr. C. H. COLES ...	11/9/17	Gr. T. H. GARWOOD...	12/9/17
Gr. A. G. DEANE ...	11/9/17	Gr. J. WHITELAW ...	12/9/17
Gr. A. DAUCY ...	11/9/17	Gr. R. A. HILL ...	27/4/17
Gr. H. DIAPER ...	11/9/17	Bdr. F. ECKERSLEY ...	27/4/17
Gr. W. C. EVANS ...	11/9/17	Gr. T. P. CRAIG ...	30/4/17
Gr. A. ELSON ...	11/9/17	Gr. H. PRESTON ...	30/4/17
Gr. F. T. EDWARDS ...	11/9/17	Gr. D. JONES... ...	30/12/17
Gr. G. FERGUSON ...	11/9/17	Gr. W. GOMM ...	31/1/18
Gr. B. S. FERGUSON...	11/9/17	Gr. J. DUNCAN ...	12/3/18
Gr. S. FELLOWS ...	11/9/17	Bdr. D. B. ROSS ...	21/3/18
Gr. J. GIBSON ...	11/9/17	Cpl. H. McNAUGHTON	21/3/18
Gr. P. BRIEN... ...	12/9/17	Gr. J. S. HANNAN ...	21/3/18

N.C.O.'s and Men—*continued*.

NAME.	DATE.	NAME.	DATE.
Gr. J. S. Oxley	21/3/18	Bdr. J. M. Smith	18/9/18
Gr. F. Cooper	26/3/18	Gr. H. Lovering	18/9/18
Gr. H. Mugleston	5/4/18	Gr. S. Passingham	18/9/18
Gr. W. Handley	7/6/18	Gr. A. S. Gardiner	18/9/18
Gr. L. Burnett	5/7/18	Gr. R. Lumsden	18/9/18
Gr. P. Kenna	30/7/17	Gr. D. J. Jones	19/9/18
Gr. J. Ward	18/9/18	Gr. R. M. Cochran	19/9/18
Gr. T. D. M. Wallace	18/9/18	Gr. A. G. Whitelaw	19/9/18
Gr. A. Underwood	18/9/18	Gr. L. W. Jackson	19/9/18
Gr. S. F. G. Pearson	18/9/18	Gr. C. Harwood	19/9/18
Gr. W. Philp	18/9/18	Gr. J. Turner	18/9/18
Gr. C. W. Johnson	18/9/18	Gr. R. T. Kensey	19/9/18
Gr. W. D. Pope	18/9/18	Gr. J. Turfus	18/9/18
Gr. A. H. Kerr	18/9/18	Gr. J. Arnold	19/9/18
Sgt. J. Black	18/9/18	Gr. H. J. Tobin	19/9/18
Cpl. B. Dalrymple	18/9/18	Sgt. G. Graves	6/10/18
Cpl. J. Anderson	18/9/18		

CIVILISATION AGAIN

PASSING through Bony we travelled to Hervilly, stopping there the night and going on next morning to Le Mesnil, where we found quarters in an old rest camp for a few days. On October 16th the journey was continued to Peronne, where train was taken for the north. Passing Chaulnes, Villers-Brettonneux, Amiens, and Doullens, the Battery was deposited at a small place called Fouquereuil on the 17th, and after spending some hours on rest there, mounted the lorries again and went *via* Bethune and Noeux-les-Mines to the conjoined villages of Petit Sains and Sains-en-Gohelle. In many ways this district provided a strong contrast to our recent experiences. The houses were well built, the streets well kept, and the people were clean and prosperous-looking. Here lived the coal miners who worked in the mines near by, and their daily round appeared to be little disturbed by the war, though the distant flashes at night reminded us that fighting was still going on. The 21st saw us once more on board the lorries, and we left the quiet village, passing through Noeux-les-Mines and turning east to cross our old front line at La Bassee. The journey ended at a village called Wavrin, on the Bethune-Lille railway, and the main billet there was a large mansion which had previously been occupied by the enemy. Wavrin had been badly shelled and bombed ; roads had been mined and houses blown up, but during our stay a few of the inhabitants ventured to return and were rationed with the Battery. At this place it was gradually revealed to us that we were once more going up the line, but on this occasion it was the railway line. Parties of about 50 men were detailed daily to join the R.E.'s, who were repairing the permanent way ; and, leaving the howitzers under the village trees, they marched off to the new job. The line had been damaged in a very thorough fashion ; trench mortar shells had been used on culverts and bridges, and at every junction of the rails the head of a stick bomb had been exploded. Uncomplimentary remarks were made about the ballast, the rails, the sleepers, and the fish-plates, while a suggestion that " Jerry " prisoners should be put on the job hardly received the attention it deserved. After a short apprenticeship with the shovel, these promising workers were permitted to carry rails, next to use the box spanners, and finally to assist with the eight-pound hammer and " jim crow."

Meanwhile the advance of the army continued ; the observation balloons were far away on the horizon, and the Gothas ceased from troubling. A single line was put through at Santes and Don, and while at the former station we saw the great concrete pit and steel arc for the gun which, the French people said, had been destroyed by a bomb from a British aeroplane. About this time the formal entry of our troops into Lille took place, and on November 1st a party of men from the Battery paid a visit there. After four years under the Boche, with little food, under constant threats of imprisonment and fines, subject to daily visits of inspection, and having been deprived of all reserves of foodstuffs, the people of the city welcomed the British with enthusiasm, and from now to the end of the year we paid many visits to the French Manchester. It was during this period that the problem of Lille money was encountered. During the occupation of this territory paper money and paper coins had been printed more or less under German dictation, and certain shops and canteens refused this doubtful currency, but eventually arrangements were made for its replacement by notes of the Bank of France, and the cry of " *no bon* " died away.

On November 2nd the Battery moved to Fretin, continuing work on the railway line, through Lesquin to Templeuve, Nomain, and Orchies, and travelling to and fro by lorry when the work lay at a distance. The village had one main street about a mile long, running at right angles to the railway, and at a farm in the Rue de Templeuve the headquarters of the Battery were situated. The billets call for little comment, except that on the whole it was more comfortable outside than in, but the people of the village were very hospitable, and armed with half-a-dozen words of French it was easy to make friends. Every house was, as usual, labelled as a German billet, but the boys over fifteen and men under sixty had been forced to accompany the retreating enemy into Belgium. The natives had been made to work at repairing the roads and tilling the fields, to gather nettles, apparently for making some kind of cloth, and to hand over all objects of copper or brass which they possessed. The girls of the village had to attend a parade every morning for work in the fields, and anyone absent without a certificate from the Boche military doctor was fined or imprisoned. A similar penalty was imposed if in the street men civilians omitted to salute the officers or if the women did not say " Good day." Electric light was installed in all billets, and for this the occupier paid three francs per month. Permission to visit relatives in neighbouring villages was almost invariably refused, and it was no wonder that the phrase most often heard among the people was " *Les sales bêtes !*" Now French soldiers who had been completely shut off from their homes for four years were welcomed back once more, and other families heard for the first time that their men folk would never return.

The Parisian papers came regularly to the village, and the progress of the enemy retirement was carefully followed, but we had an unexpected shock on the 8th November, when the Battery received orders to go into action, and the Major went forward to choose a position. Two hours later the order was cancelled, the enemy having relinquished his hold during the night and gone back some miles. The subject which now became of highest importance was the armistice, and all the moves leading up to its signing by the enemy were fully discussed in the public meeting held daily at the cook-house. On the fateful morning of November 11th a padre marching along behind some infantry was seen excitedly waving his walking-stick, but no one took much notice of him. Then somebody said that a French soldier had rushed into a house shouting " *La guerre est finie,*" but still we doubted. Soon afterwards a notice was posted on the barn door officially stating that the armistice would take effect from 11 o'clock that morning. Then the Battery picked up sides and played a game of football.

Wild rumours now became current about some ceremonial return to England, and many members of the Battery who had failed to win laurels on the railway line made a very promising start as novelists. It soon became evident that the Battery would not be moving into Germany with

our advancing army, and after work on the railway at
Orchies had ceased for a few days, orders to pack up were
given, and the whole Brigade moved on the 27th November
to a village called Phalempin, some twelve kilometres distant.
Here we occupied a large chateau and its outbuildings, while
the guns were parked just opposite the main entrance.   As
at Fretin the niceties of mounting guard were here ex-
haustively studied, and the usual morning routine was
carried out.   Later on this was varied by salvaging and
police duty, but even these delights failed to remove the
general atmosphere of boredom which at first prevailed.
The prospect of leave produced a little animation, and the
old argument which begins "If two warrants come in to-
morrow" was heard over and over again.   Football flour-
ished, and many vigorous inter-battery contests took place.

The railway station, as well as some houses and roads,
had been blown up in Phalempin, and when the British
troops were known to be advancing, all the villagers for
some obscure reason had to leave for Templeuve, about
17 kilometres distant.   The sick and aged had to be taken
on wheelbarrows, and a few portable belongings were also
removed.   For three weeks the villagers were away, and
on their return found their dwellings rifled and all their stock
of winter vegetables taken away by the Boche.   Thus they
were worse off than the folks at Fretin, who had taken
shelter in cellars, and afterwards emerged to greet our
incoming troops.   In both villages food was controlled by
a local committee, and the prices of rationed commodities
were very high.   In the Battery during the early days of
December the educational scheme which was heard of at
Warloy appeared in a different and more workable form,
but it stood little chance against the increasing probability
of demobilisation, and the attractions of the cinema opened
in the village under the auspices of the Australians.

On Christmas Eve there was a slight fall of snow, and
still more seasonable was the hearty carol-singing in the
dining-hall, audible all over the chateau grounds.   The
Catering Committee, under Lieut. Pinder, had done its
work well, and the 25th started with eggs and bacon for
breakfast.   At 10.45 a.m. there was " pay up," and at 11.45
a.m. Church parade.   Dinner was arranged for 4 p.m.,

and its preparation was carried out by Mess and Battery cooks, who had joined forces.   There was ample room for the whole unit in the large loft, where tables, forms, stoves, and a piano had been installed, and a squad of willing workers under Corporal T. Clarke had decorated this dining-hall with flags, ivy, and coloured paper chains, while illumination was provided by Chinese lanterns and hurricane lamps.   The menu was as follows :—

Soup.

Roast Beef.   Roast Mutton.

Potatoes.   Carrots.

Christmas Pudding,
with Whisky Sauce.

Blanc-mange and Custard.

Fruit and Nuts.   Beer, Rum, Lime Juice, Ginger Ale

At intervals there were short impromptu speeches mingled with good-humoured chaff.   The Major opened the proceedings with a short speech, and later the Captain summed up the occasion with " Probably this is the last time we shall have the pleasure of meeting together under these conditions "—(A Voice : " We hope so.")—and went on to wish the company a happy resumption of civilian life. The Quarter then declaimed in great style the Royal Artillery toast :—

> We have no gaudy colours, boys,
> To flap before the wind,
> No music to remind us
> Of the girls we've left behind ;
> But when we are in battle,
> Why, that's the time to see
> The ragged-tailed old blighters
> Of the Royal Artillery.

And the Sergeant-Major gave " We've worked together and fought together, and now we'll drink together."   There was no hesitation in complying.

At 6 p.m. the Major announced " Rum up," and the ceremony commenced to the stimulating chorus :—

> If you want the Quarter
> We know where he is,
> If you want the Quarter
> We know where he is,
> Mopping up the buckshee rum.

The concert then began, under Quarter-Master E. E. Biggs as stage-manager. The costumes were by His Britannic Majesty's Government ; the scenery by Messrs. Clark, Phalempin & Co.; the music by " Horace," and the lyrics by officers and men of the Battery.

So we spent Christmas, 1918—we who had been through rough and smooth together—and looked forward to coming home. Some were absent from that gathering for whom there was no home-coming. They are at rest.

Ready to start civil life afresh, we centred our hopes in 1919, the year of the Peace.

*   *   *   *   *   *   *

Our story would be incomplete did we not pay a tribute to the kindness of the ladies of the Forth R.G.A. Comforts Fund and of Miss A. E. Harbourne, of Dungarvan, who so regularly sent comforts and cigarettes to the men of the Battery. The parcels always arrived when they were most needed, and ever met with a warm reception.

NOMINAL ROLL OF BATTERY AT THE COMMENCEMENT OF DEMOBILISATION

Officers.

Major G. H. Cooke, M.C.
Capt. A. K. Smith.
Lt. F. Dewhurst.
2/Lt. J. A. Nicholson.

2/Lt. S. G. May.
2/Lt. R. F. Pinder.
2/Lt. H. O. Lydford.
2/Lt. H. L. Johnston, M.C.

Warrant Officers, N.C.O.'s and Men.

B.S.M. M. O'Hara.
B.Q.M.S. E. E. Biggs.
Sgt. J. Johnston.
Sgt. B. Mundell.
Sgt. J. A. Ellerton.
Sgt. A. Garven.
Sgt. B. Dalrymple.
Staff-Sgt. G. Brown.
Cpl. T. M. Clark.
Cpl. J. Anderson.
Sig.-Cpl. W. Thirlwell.
Cpl. H. Clench.
Cpl. D. B. Allan.
Cpl. A. J. Pym.
Bdr. D. Wood.
Bdr. R. Leach.
Bdr. R. P. Boon.
Bdr. T. Whitelaw.
Sig. Bdr. F. G. Povey.
Bdr. I. T. Williams.
Bdr. A. E. Duckworth.
Bdr. J. Whitelaw.
Bdr. W. Stone.
Bdr. R. Stewart.
Bdr. W. A. Williams.
Bdr. R. Lamond.
Sig.-Bdr. A. Ashdown.
Staff-Gnr. A. Dore.
Staff-Gnr. H. Sayer.
W.-Gnr. J. Walker.
Gnr. F. Alsop.
Gnr. W. K. Andrews.
Gnr. J. Ashwick.
Sig. A. J. Bain.
Gnr. W. N. Bates.
Sig. J. T. Beddon.

Sig. H. Beel.
Gnr. H. E. Best.
Gnr. P. T. H. Bird.
Sig. J. H. Bowden.
Gnr. P. Bradburn.
Sig. S. Brine.
Gnr. C. E. Brookes.
Gnr. F. Button.
Gnr. W. Carr.
Gnr. T. Carruthers.
Gnr. B. Carter.
Gnr. S. Churchill.
Sig. B. Cocker.
Gnr. J. H. Coombe.
Gnr. R. Craig.
Gnr. R. Cutt.
Gnr. A. Davidson.
Gnr. F. T. Edwards.
Gnr. A. Eustice.
Gnr. F. Fenton.
Gnr. A. Fraser.
Sig. W. A. Fraser.
Gnr. E. A. Garland.
Gnr. B. G. E. Golding.
Gnr. J. W. Gosley.
Gnr. H. Hall.
Gnr. W. Handley.
Gnr. F. Hebdon.
Gnr. J. Hine.
Gnr. J. H. Hirst.
Sig. R. Hoare.
Gnr. R. Hollands.
Sig. H. Horsfall.
Sig. F. Hull.
Gnr. H. Jacobs.
Gnr. J. L. Jaggard.

Warrant Officers, N.C.O.'s and Men—*continued.*

Sig. D. Jenkins.
Gnr. D. Johnston.
Gnr. B. L. Kendall.
Gnr. R. T. Kensey.
Gnr. A. King.
Sig. J. King.
Gnr. J. Kinsella.
Gnr. J. Kirkup.
Gnr. W. C. Lake.
Gnr. J. A. Lansdown.
Gnr. W. Large.
Gnr. G. Laverick.
Sig. C. Leadbeater.
Gnr. J. Lee.
Gnr. A. E. Lewis.
Gnr. A. W. Little.
Gnr. H. Little.
Gnr. J. Little.
Gnr. J. Lockett.
Gnr. B. Lucas.
Gnr. H. W. Lyes.
Gnr. R. McDonald.
Sig. R. R. McGregor.
Gnr. A. Mills.
Gnr. W. H. Mitchell.
Gnr. J. Muir.
Gnr. W. A. Neill.
Gnr. J. Neill.
Sig. J. P. Oliver.

Gnr. W. H. P. Osborne.
Gnr. F. C. Parkinson.
Sig. W. H. Parsons.
Gnr. G. Phillips.
Gnr. W. Phipps.
Gnr. F. Plowman.
Gnr. A. Powers.
Gnr. H. Punton.
Gnr. A. S. Rae.
Gnr. H. Rawnsley.
Gnr. H. R. Robertson.
Gnr. G. H. Salt.
Gnr. J. H. Scudder.
Gnr. P. Shean.
Gnr. R. Skeates.
Sig. B. Smith.
Gnr. J. Strath.
Gnr. H. A. Taylor.
Gnr. W. H. Thomason.
Gnr. R. V. Venner.
Gnr. H. Walmsley.
Sig. A. Walshaw.
Sig. E. C. Walter.
Sig. E. A. Webber.
Sig. J. J. Webber.
Gnr. A. G. Whitelaw.
Gnr. L. Williams.
Sig. A. E. Wilkinson.
Gnr. J. C. Wilson.

178 SIEGE BATTERY R.G.A., PHALEMPIN, DECEMBER 31 1918

DIARY OF CHIEF EVENTS

1916.

June 16.	Battery established on authority from War Office.
July 3.	Advance party arrived at King's Park, Edinburgh.
,, 5.	Main body arrived at King's Park from Firth of Forth Defences.
,, 20.	Bere Island signallers from Bexhill-on-Sea arrived at Edinburgh.
,, 28.	Left Edinburgh for Ramillies Barracks, Aldershot.
Sept. 18.	Left Aldershot for firing course at Larkhill, Salisbury Plain.
,, 22.	Arrived Stockcross Camp, Newbury, for mobilisation.
Oct. 8.	Embarked Southampton for Le Havre.
,, 9.	Disembarked at Le Havre.
,, 11.	Entrained at Le Havre for unknown destination.
,, —.	Detrained at Savy, in Arras Sector.
,, 13.	Occupied position near Dainville.
Nov. 18.	Occupied position near Berneville, on Arras-Doullens road.
Dec. 24.	Moved to new position off Arras—St. Pol road near Anzin St. Aubin.
,, 25.	Christmas Day. Bully and biscuits.

1917.

Jan. 6.	Daylight raid by our troops near Blangy. Battery fired its first complete bombardment programme.
,, 31.	Shelled heavily with 5·9's.
April 4.	Bombardment for battle of Arras began.
,, 9.	Barrage 5.30 a.m., and grand attack launched. Battery moved forward to position in our original front line in Blangy.
,, 10 to 13.	Snow blizzards. Constant firing to support attacks on Monchy-le-Preux.
,, 14.	Moved forward and took position on Tilloy-Wancourt road.
,, 16.	Attacks renewed. Heavy programmes, averaging 700 rounds per day, carried out.
,, 30.	Moved forward to position in open fields near Wancourt.
May 3.	Battle reopened. Heavy programme fired.
,, 15.	Right section went to camp on Arras—St. Pol road for four days' rest.
,, 19.	Left Section relieved by Right Section. Two guns in action.
June 3.	Occupied position in Happy Valley, near Wancourt.
,, 25.	Advance party left for Ypres.

July	1.	Right Section, with two guns, left for Ypres.
,,	2.	Entrained at Savy for Abeele.
,,	4.	Arrived at Asylum Corner, Ypres. Billets obtained in Vlamertinghe.
,,	5.	Leave started.
,,	10.	Leave stopped.
,.	31.	Third battle of Ypres opened. Heavy programme fired.
Aug.	16.	Battle re-opened.
,,	24.	Moved forward to position behind the Vinery, near St. Jean.
Sept.	11.	Many gas casualties caused to men on guns.
Oct.	4.	Attack renewed by Australians. Battery carried out a very heavy programme ; 15 Siege Battery took over two guns.
,,	5.	Relief off duty entrained at Poperinghe.
,,	6.	Occupied position at Frezenburg. Battery supported attack on Arras Sector.
,,	20.	Party from Ypres arrived at Wancourt.
,,	24.	Advance party left Wancourt for new position on Henin—St. Leger road.
,,	28.	Guns pulled in at new position.
Nov.	14.	Battery moved by road *via* Bapaume for unknown destination.
,,	15.	Occupied position in sunken road near Havrincourt Wood.
,,	20.	Battle of Cambrai opened.
,,	23.	Battery took up forward position in Demicourt.
,,	30.	Enemy counter attack. Battery heavily shelled. Retired to new position in Hermies.
Dec.	25.	Christmas Day celebrated at Havrincourt Wood.

1918.

Jan.	7.	Battery pulled out for a rest, and made journey by road to Maricourt.
,,	8.	Journey continued. Stayed at Forceville.
.,	9.	Arrived at Beauval, near Doullens.
,,	13.	Battery sports.
,,	28.	Good-bye, civilisation. Battery entrained at Doullens.
,,	29.	Took up position off Fins-Gouzeaucourt road.
Feb.	9.	Battery nearly had a bath at Metz.
,,	26.	Right Section occupied position in Hermies.
,,	27.	Left Section moved to Hermies.
Mar.	12.	Battery position heavily shelled with gas shells.
,,	21.	Great enemy attack opened. Battery position very heavily shelled all day.
,,	22.	Hermies position evacuated 2 a.m. Retired to Neuville. Guns afterwards saved and taken to Rocquigny.
,,	23.	Guns in action at Rocquigny. Retired to Albert.

Mar.	24.	Battery went forward, and was in action near Contal-maison.
,,	25.	Retired to position west of Albert. Went forward again and took position near Fricourt. Retired again to east of Albert.
,,	26.	Retreated to position west of Millencourt. Enemy heavily engaged whilst advancing on Albert. Retired to Warloy, and again went forward to Millencourt.
,,	27.	Retired to position east of Warloy.
,,	29.	Occupied position at north-eastern corner of Henencourt Wood.
April	2.	Battery heavily shelled. Moved to position behind Henencourt Wood.
,,	17.	Left Section occupied position in Senlis Valley.
,,	24.	Enemy attack renewed. Battery position heavily shelled.
June	5.	Right Section took up position in Senlis Valley.
July	2.	Handed over guns to 225 Siege Battery, and took over their guns in position west of Millencourt. " Spanish Influenza " epidemic broke out.
Aug.	22.	Allied offensive opened on the Albert sector.
,,	24.	Moved to Bouzincourt.
,,	25.	Moved to position on Albert-Méaulte road near Vivier Mill.
,,	26.	Occupied position in Mametz.
,,	29.	Battery in action at Guillemont. Heavily shelled.
Sept.	2.	Battery in position near Combles.
,,	3.	Battery in action on Bapaume-Peronne road near Sailly Saillisel.
,,	5.	Moved to Manancourt.
,,	6.	Moved to Equancourt.
,,	7.	Occupied position near Sorel-le-Grand.
,,	9.	Battery out of action for a few days' rest at Equancourt.
,,	12.	In action again at Sorel-le-Grand. Shelled heavily, and took up new position near Saulcourt.
,,	26.	Occupied position in Railway Bank near Epehy. Forty-eight hours' bombardment of Hindenburg Line begun.
,,	28.	Battery moved forward to battle position east of Ronssoy.
,,	29.	Attack on Hindenburg Line.
Oct.	4.	Battery crossed Hindenburg Line at 'Bony, and took up position behind Railway Ridge.
,,	6.	Guns in position east of Gouy.
,,	8.	Battery supports the attack on Serain.
,,	10.	Battery pulled out and rested in billets in Hindenburg Line.
,,	12.	Battery went on rest. Camped at Hervilly.

Oct. 13. Arrived at Le Mesnil.

,, 16. Left Le Mesnil and entrained at Peronne.

,, 17. Detrained at Fouquereuil, near Bethune, and went by road to Petit Sains.

,, 21. Left Petit Sains and took billets in Wavrin.

Nov. 2. Battery moved to Fretin.

,, 11. Armistice declared.

,, 27. Battery moved to Phalempin.

Dec. 14. Demobilisation commences. Three men leave for England.

,, 25. Christmas Day. Battery dinner.

J. K. and I. T. W.

"STANDING EASY"

GUNNER ARTEMAS

In the night—in the rainy, cold, and windy night-time—there was I, Artemas, in the huggy near the guns.

And because of the fury of the elements, neither I nor my brethren were desirous of putting so much as the end of the nose outside the huggy.

Not because the lodging was good, for it was grievously afflicted with rats and divers other beasts, but because the night was foul and we would fain sleep.

Nevertheless before we had slumbered for the space of fifteen minutes there fell upon our ears a sound like unto that of a foghorn, or, as another saith, like the cry of a bullock which alasseth for his poor brother.

And when we came to ourselves we said one to another, It is surely action. And it was so.

Then turned we out, speaking of our king and country, but not after the manner of recruiting posters.

Weird words spake we in wrath, Gaelic and Erse and other language, each according to his ability and without repetition.

Grievous was the plight of our brother who sought his gun by way of the flooded shell-hole, so that his plaint exceeded ours in vigour, and we hearkened unto him as unto a master.

Yet the voice of our complaining reached not unto the commander of the battery, nor did his heart soften towards us.

Rather did his anger quicken, so that he spake sharply over the telephone asking if the Battery were ready unto battle.

But he at the section post answered only, Shake up.

Then said the commander, enquire of Sergeant Johnston whether the guns be ready unto battle.

Thereupon spake the sergeant, who was come thither, Yea yea, sir, even now are they in the line.

Then answered he, Let there be three rounds of gun fire, having an interval therewith of ten minutes.

Then were the voices of the gunners raised anew ; though by reason of the heavy going and the heaving all together, they were scant of breath.

Other targets did the Brigade send unto the commander of the Battery, and when the sergeant, near the 'phone, lifted his voice to cry Fresh target, those who bore the burthen of the shells sang their ditties in a loud voice and were disrespectfully funny.

Nevertheless, in spite of the grousing, the Boche lacked not his iron rations, and according to the commandment of the officer, when two of 101E had been sent forth, then followed after them one 106, so that the enemy sought in haste his caverns in the bowels of the earth.

Then came one of the Army Service Corps to the sergeant by the guns, saying, Lo, here be three lorry loads of ammunition. Prithee unload them quickly, for my desire is to return to my kip.

Then the gunners carried to the guns provision for the morrow.

And when they desired to enquire of the driver concerning the number of projectiles he had brought, Lo, the driver had fled.

So passed the night, and when the day had dawned the men lifted their eyes unto the cook-house.

And seeing Rhondda, the food controller, waving his hand unto them, they said, Dam good, and went thither with their dixies.

Bacon and bread and dip gave he unto them, nor of good hot tea did he stint them.

Unshaven and smutty of countenance they consumed their provender, joking with cheerful voices, prophesying the date of the commencement of leave, and asking one of another whether the army were winning.

After this manner, then, for the behoof of their inquiring posterity, did the Garrison Artillery do in the Great War.

J. J. W.

BELOW ZERO

Digging in the mud, in the chalk, and in the rock,
  Oh ! Gaw blimey aint it cold ?
When you go for tea, you get tea and N.C. Toc,
  Oh ! Gaw blimey aint it cold ?
With this is jam and biscuits,
Or sometimes jam and bread ;
And when there is a change at all
It's bread and jam instead ;
If we ever catch the Kaiser
We'll break his——nuff said ;
  Oh ! Gaw blimey aint it cold ?

Going into action on a dark and murky night,
  Oh ! Gaw blimey aint it cold ?
You cannot find the rammer nor yet the dial-sight,
  Oh ! Gaw blimey aint it cold ?
You stumble, slip and curse,
For the night is thick and black ;
But you find a shell at last
And it goes in with a clack ;
The Boche gets iron rations
And you get shrapnel back ;
  Oh ! Gaw blimey aint it cold ?

Walking down the road to the nine o'clock parade,
  Oh ! Gaw blimey aint it cold ?
Walking down the road with a shovel and a spade,
  Oh ! Gaw blimey aint it cold ?
You want the Sergeant-Major,
The Quarter comes instead ;
You want the Ord'ly Sergeant,
The devil's still in bed ;
Sighing for a tot of rum,
You wish that you were dead ;
  Oh ! Gaw blimey aint it cold ?

Waiting at the cook-house, waiting in a queue,
  Oh ! Gaw blimey aint it cold ?
Water and an onion, altho' they call it stew,
  Oh ! Gaw blimey aint it cold ?
To make it slightly thicker
There's oatmeal at the door,
And you will not want your lid for
" There's no rice in this corps ; "
A detachment lives on rations
That's not enough for four ;
  Oh ! Gaw blimey aint it cold ?

                              I. T. W.

THE TRUTH ABOUT OUR OFFICERS

BY ONE OF 'EM.

BETWEEN you and me the officers of our Mess are not at all what the other ranks think they are, or the public in general expects them to be. I know the popular idea of an officer is a man with a lisp or drawl, who does more to nullify the splendid fighting of our gallant men in the battle line than the combined efforts of the hostile armies. Nothing of the sort, I assure you. A finer, more sterling lot of fellows than our officers it would be difficult to find on the earth, in the heavens above or the waters beneath. When I think of some of their wonderful attainments words fail me. Unfortunately, as with all great minds, those qualities which would excite the envy and admiration of ' all men are so carefully camouflaged from the vulgar gaze that the mere mortal not in the know goes away with the impression that a more ordinary set of uniformed incompetents never existed.

This is a pity ; a wrong idea is, of course, created, to dispel which necessitates my exclusive services. Take the Major, for example. If ever you were lucky enough to put your head round the door of our mess probably the first sight that would catch your eye would be the figure of our O.C. sitting in the only comfortable chair in the mess, coyly puffing away at a Turkish cigarette whilst he studies his hand. Observe the furrows on his noble brow as he cogitates whether he shall make a no-trump call or play policeman. Then remark upon the masterly way in which he will finesse through his opponents. It is a thrilling sight, and one instinctively feels that here at least is the brain that can counter the wiliest strokes of the most cunning adversary.

Nor is auction bridge his only ambition. He will sit for hours at a stretch working through the problems of " Patience " and other high-brow card games. Or again, watch him calmly stand on his head in a corner of the room. I must admit that when he commenced to practise this hair-raising feat I had qualms about the success of the venture. I should have known better. By assiduous persistence and severe casualties to the plaster on the wall the whole objective was eventually attained. It was a touching sight to witness the first accomplishment of this extraordinary feat ; there was none of that cold, frigid dignity that marks the shallow mind. On the contrary, with an almost childlike enthusiasm he puffed out his chest and tears welled up into his eyes. Some of the fellows said they were due to exertion, but I knew better. What more fitting example could one have of true greatness ? As some clever man once so adequately phrased it, "A man with a will of iron, but the heart of a little child."

As a matter of fact, I could write reams on this gallant Irish gentleman, but there are the other officers to consider, so I reluctantly dismiss him to make room for the Skipper. The latter is not so named because of his affinity for sardines, although in the very early days of my green subalternship I thought that was the reason. The name is merely an endearing term used for captains—more evidence of the ready wit that is displayed in the commissioned service, proving to some extent my original claim for officers.

As I insinuated, the Skipper is not named after any brand of sardines, but I must admit that he is remarkably fond of that particular delicacy. In fact, there are few men who have so expert a knowledge of the flavours of such various comestibles as curries, shrimps, prawns, sardines, pickles, sauce, and cheese. The Skipper hails from the east, and is a bit of an enigma. Unlike some of the other members, he talks very little, and therefore must think a great deal. He also parts his hair very nicely indeed ; not that he is effeminate in any way ; rather the reverse. He once told me he was a believer in early rising and cold baths. In fact, he is credited with taking a cold bath every morning, although during the months of December, January, and February I have a shrewd suspicion that his bath-water comes off the French stove, but that, I understand, is merely to thaw the ice, which is always unpleasant. He also performs some remarkable gymnastic evolutions before dressing, which probably explains why he is usually rather late at breakfast. Courteous and reserved, he is nevertheless very human. Wild horses would not make him accept

the third light off one match, which is striking evidence
of the emotional characteristics of this great man. In those
rare intervals of leisure which he allows himself he shows
that by nature he is an ardent collector of picture post-cards,
and at all times I have found him untiring in this harmless
and intellectual pursuit. But I think that sufficient has
been written about the simple manly virtues of our second-
in-command to need no apology for bringing the First Loot
to your notice.

Our First Loot is a very profound gentleman, well
versed in English literature and French history. I can
assure you his scholastic abilities are of no mean order,
and he is also one of the most obliging officers one could
wish to meet. He can read a French newspaper equally
with those of his own tongue, and willingly translates to
us any passages that meet with his approval. Only once
have I had reason to doubt his knowledge of the language
of our Allies. It happened in a certain café where I had
observed a charming young French lady, and wishing to
learn her views on the Boche I asked the First Loot to act
as interpreter for me. Unfortunately there was a hitch
somewhere in his translation of my polite inquiries, for
before I knew where I was I found he had invited the lady
to dine with me. The dinner cost me well over a hundred
francs. Our First Loot said it was a *faux pas* ; what my
wife will call it if she ever gets to hear about the matter
heaven only knows !

In private life the First Loot is a Government official,
consequently his energy is tremendous. His brain power
is also very high, and his initiative in getting the easiest
chair is something to witness. Do not run away with the
idea that he is not a champion in sport. As a ping-pong
player he is difficult to match, and he has been known to
challenge a certain officer to a contest in more than one
manly sport. Apart from all this, he is credited with being
a very wonderful connoisseur of the continental vintages.

If I could only write all I wish about the bunch of Junior
Subalterns who have graced our mess there would be some
surprising matters to record, but the Editor politely informs
me that my versatile powers are confined to an article,
not a volume. Anyhow they are a remarkable lot of fellows ;

ask any of the batmen if you don't believe me. There is the Mess Secretary, for instance ; he is not very old, but the way that young fellow manipulates my money places him alongside the great financial magnates of the Empire. Each month he hands me a bill for messing which fills me at once with wonder and consternation. A paltry hundred francs or so from me he treats with as little concern as if it were a few sous. He is one of those men who think in millions, and if he ever leaves the army I predict a great future for him, either as Chancellor of the Exchequer or controller of some great Government department.

Then there is Ludendorff—we call him Ludendorff on account of his very fierce moustachios, which are the envy of the whole mess. What this brilliant officer does not know about football, railways, engineering, or education is not worth knowing. He is another great genius who talks little but thinks much, and he has a remarkably dulcet voice when he sings.

The latest addition to our mess comes from Canada, and this sturdy young Colonial brought a breath of the pines with him. Very handsome in appearance, he would be a great favourite with the ladies if it were not for his innate modesty. He is also addicted to singing during the evening, and the fine timbre of his sonorous voice can be heard at a great distance.

Everybody was sorry when X left us for Brigade. His cool daring at Poker and Bridge impressed all who were fortunate enough to meet him—a man of action, somewhat terse of speech, but a very convivial fellow at all times, though a stern believer in discipline. This splendid fellow was also a great moralist, and it is well known how he gravely censured a French estaminet keeper for her too lavish provision of wine for the troops during the critical days of the war.

Then there was Nick, who also went to Brigade. He had grey hair and a heart of eighteen, and was ever watchful over the destinies of our army. The officers have good cause to remember his welcome " buzz " on the O.P. telephone between midnight and early dawn to synchronise watches.

Jacko left us to take the post of Second-in-Command of

another battery, and I must say that this genial and outspoken officer was much missed. He was another of those convivial and sociable fellows who would never allow his comrade to take a drink without his personal support. This gentleman probably stimulated more energy in the ranks than any other officer in the Battery, and the enthusiasm amongst the men on hearing of his higher appointment will perhaps better convey the great regard in which they held him, than any words of mine.

Who will ever forget Jimmie ? He was another of our brilliant fellowship taken away from us for higher work— a Scot of Scotsmen, not without humour. Like Nick, he also kept wakeful guard over the mess, and his curious excursions in the dead of night were a source of admiration to us all. Anyone who has listened to Jimmie's wonderful lectures on fundamental principles, the survival of the fittest, or tariff reform will remember with what breadth of thought and wise toleration he set forth the pros and cons of these great questions. Not that he was one of those superior, serious persons. He was as gay a dog as any of us when occasion demanded, and his geniality under trying circumstances was more than appreciated. He could render "Annie Laurie " at times with such pathos that tears would well up in our eyes, and afterwards would tell a funny story that would set the mess rocking with laughter. Yes, we all missed Jimmie very much.

I think I have written more than sufficient to convince the greatest sceptic of the admirable qualities of the commissioned ranks. Imagine that sceptic's thoughts as he reads of the last but by no means least of our noble fraternity, the Column Officer ; with humility I must admit that a more reverent pen than mine should deal with this noble veteran of the " old contemptibles." No wonder, with such examples as this before them, that the War Office should gravely decide to prefix A.S.C. with the title *Royal*. This hero of Mons and other furious onslaughts of the terrible war is justly proud of his active service. One of the first to fling his whole strength into the world-conflict, he is one of the last to leave it, which will show you the sublime thoroughness with which he does his work. Nor does the enormous strain that this meticulous care imposes upon

H

his system ever worry or disconcert him, for he has frequently been heard to exclaim that " This is a *bon* war " in the cheeriest voice imaginable. Like the rest of the officers, his virtues are not confined to mere military matters. There are few men with such a broad knowledge of commerce, politics, sport, or religion as our Column Officer, and his discourses on high finance frequently leave us aghast. I am afraid he occasionally talks over our heads, but if he ever takes up literature his works will become classics I feel sure, years hence.

But the Editor again politely informs me that my pen has already wandered beyond the extreme limit, so I will say no more, except to humbly express the hope that these wayward words of mine will cause the scoffer to think twice before he again traduces the commissioned ranks of our Great Army.

S. G. M.

THE RUMOUR

Time, 2 p.m.

First Officer : So you've heard from your brother ?
Second Officer : Yes. He is just out of hospital, but his wife has been out of sorts, and he says in his letter (*Gunner passes within hearing*), " We are going to Southampton very shortly (*Gunner passes out of hearing*), and shall probably stay there for a month."

Time, 2.5 p.m.

Gunner to Gunner No. 2 : I believe we're on the move again soon, Bill. As I was passing just now I heard Dewsmith tell Mayford that the Battery was going to England and landing at Southampton.

Time, 2.10 p.m.

Gunner No. 2 to Signaller : Have you heard anything about this move ?
Signaller : No.
Gunner No. 2 : Well, it's right enough ; we're going to England next week—landing at Southampton.
Signaller : I heard them arguing in the office about the train accommodation we had when we came up from Havre, so perhaps there's something in it.

Time, 2.30 p.m.

Signaller to Gunner No. 3 : Have you heard the news, Tom ? We're off to England next Thursday ; going by train to Le Havre and crossing to Southampton. I'm going to try and get a new tunic from the Quarter now.

Time, 3 p.m.

Gunner No. 5 : Did Kingy get any stuff for the canteen to-day ?
Gunner No. 4 : No, he could not get anything. But it doesn't matter much, we shan't be here much longer.
Gunner No. 5 : Who said so ?
Gunner No. 4 : What ! haven't you heard the news ? The signallers have got hold of it, and they generally find out these things. We're off to Blighty next week—going by train to Le Havre and crossing to Southampton. The Quarter's got new rig-outs for everybody, and when Kingy went to the wholesale canteen to-day they wouldn't serve him because we're going away so soon. I reckon we shall march through London.

Time, 4 *p.m.*

Gunner No. 9 : What price to-day's news.

Gunner No. 10 : What's up now ? Stew for dinner to-morrow ?

Gunner No. 9 : No, but we're off to Blighty ; going to march through London with the guns, and the Major on horseback in front. Everybody's going to have a new rig-out, and we're going by train to Le Havre, cross to Southampton, and travel by the South Western Railway to Waterloo ; and after the procession we're all going to be demobilised.

S.O.S. (ANZIN)

A gunner had just screamed out "Action,"
  And the sentry repeated the shout ;
" Old Jimmy " came howling and swearing
  With a hurricane lamp that was out.

His uncovered head gleaming brightly,
  And braces not hitched to the mast,
In a frenzy of pent-up passion
  To the dug-outs he hurried fast.

At a gun-team dug-out he halted,
  A wild look shone in his eye ;
Down the mud-soaked steps he tottered,
  . And yelled out that blood-curdling cry.

" S.O.S. ! Come oot ! It is action !
  D'ye hear me ? Hi, mister, you !
The Boche is across at oor wire,
  And the devils they might get through ! "

The gunners in bed quietly listened
  To that voice in the cold, still night ;
" Dad " Wardle got hold of a candle,
  And bawled loudly and long for a light.

" S.O.S. ! Come oot ! It is action ! "
  Once more came the bellowing roar ;
A gunner, with boots half-frozen,
  Complained that his feet were sore.

With a leap, a rush, and a scramble
  Our "A" sub. uncovered their gun,
While " B " sub. objected to night work,
  And " C " sub. sighed softly for rum.

But " D " sub. were still in their " huggy,"
  The Sergeant in bed in a trance,
When upon them " Old Jimmy " came pouncing,
  In a fantastical sort of a dance.

" Where the hell are your men, Sergeant Stewart ?
  Turn them oot as· quick as you can ; "
The Sergeant, to save overcrowding,
  Lay in bed while the stampede began.

In an hour, · perhaps a half, maybe less, sir,
  One gunner of " D " sub. was seen
Arrayed in his gum-boots and helmet
  And a fluttering shirt in between.

By torchlight the thing was amusing,
  Each man was in strange night attire ;
" Old Jimmy," still clutching the lantern,
  Stood covered in cold slimy mire.

Though we shivered with cold in the gun-pits,
  We kept up a good rate of fire ;
S.O.S. from the trenches was answered,
  And " Jerry " was caught on the wire.

" Cover up and break off " was the order,
  The Boche his objective had lost ;
" Old Jimmy," with unconcealed gladness,
  Returned to the B.C. Post.

J. W.

VIGNETTES

GENEROSITY.

It was a time of poor rations, and the troops were famished, but hope sprang up once more when Fallowman brought a large parcel into the dug-out. He untied the string, unpacked the parcel, laid out the contents, looked at them deliberately—then repacked them carefully and fastened the box. Looking round he said, "Anybody want this bit of brown paper?"

SYMPATHY.

Late one summer afternoon a fast plane swoops across to attack the Warloy balloon. Anti-aircraft batteries fail to prevent the deed, and a little flame appears at one end of the greenish-gold casing. The band in the village smoothly plays "When you come to the end of a perfect day" as the observers leap out and their white parachutes open. The flames now have a firm hold, and the envelope is ablaze from end to end. The band gives a spirited rendering of the "Marsellaise." Now the flaming mass falls through the air with a roaring sound, strikes the earth, and gives off heavy clouds of smoke. From the village comes the sound of "God Save the King."

"GOOD-BYE, VIRGINIA."

The men of the Battery, dead tired after days of retreating, slept in the lorries. It was two o'clock in the morning, and a touch of frost could be felt in the clear, still air. Behind us, in the town of Albert, shone the lurid glare of stores fiercely burning, and from that direction came the sound of music. Down the moonlit road, headed by the band with their instruments of gleaming brass, marched the infantry. Their quick step brought them nearer, and the brisk tune roused some of our men from sleep. Then the sound gradually faded away into the distance and was heard no more.

" Private ——, Prisoner, Died of Wounds."

" There was an English prisoner," said Jeanne, " who was brought to the German Red Cross Hospital here at Phalempin. He was badly wounded, and seemed very quiet and lonely. But when night came he would listen for the British aeroplanes, and at the first sound of their engines his face would light up, and, pointing skywards, he would say to the Germans, ' Camarade up there, Fritz ; Camarade up there.' Then he was satisfied, and went to sleep. But in a little while his wound became worse, and towards the end he talked of his wife and his little children, and cried bitterly. His grave, M'sieur Jack ? It is in the little cemetery close by the aerodrome."

" X."

BATTERY SONGS

Editor's Note.—Appearance in print has given a rather anæmic character to some of the following songs, but memory will doubtless be able to remedy the shortcomings.

An old Bass bottle was washed up by the sea,
An old Bass bottle came rolling in to me,
And inside was a message with these words written on,
" Whoever finds the bottle finds the beer all gone."

In the evening by the moonlight
   You can hear the Gothas coming ;
In the evening by the moonlight
   You can hear their engines humming ;
And the boys have got the wind up,
They'll sit down the " sap " and listen,
As he bombs all the dug-outs
 By the moonlight.

Hop along, sister Mary, hop along,
Hop along, hop along ;
Hop along, sister Mary, hop along,
It will finish by and by.

Oh, that mine-sap,
Oh, that lovely mine-sap,
Oh, that mine-sap,
Come on down the sap.

Keep away from that window,
My true love and my dove,
   Keep away from that window over there ;
Call some other night,
'Cause there's going to be a fight,
   And the Gothas are a-flying in the air.

THE GOTHA.

Tune—" Sure a little bit of heaven."

Sure a great big hulking Gotha
   Flew across the sky one day,
And it hovered over Hermies
   In a Hunnish sort of way ;
And when the air scout saw him,
   Then he blew the old stand fast
To warn the battery gunners
   Not to move till Fritz had passed.
Then they peppered him with shrapnel
   Just to keep the Hun engaged,
And they gave it him so sweetly
   That the Boche gave way to rage ;
And he bombed the Battery cook-house
   And the B.C. Post as well;
And as the gunners beat it
   Sure they wished him deep in h——.

SING ME TO SLEEP.

Sing me to sleep where bullets fall,
Let me forget this war and all ;
Damp is my dug-out, damp my feet,
Nothing but bully and biscuits to eat.
Sing me to sleep where bombs explode,
And shrapnel shells are sent by the load ;
Over the sandbags Germans you'll find,
Dead Huns in front, and dead Huns behind.

CHORUS.

Far, far from Ypres I long to be,
Where German snipers can't snipe at me ;
Think of me crouching where the worms creep,
Waiting for someone to sing me to sleep.

Sing me to sleep in some old shed,
Where rats come running all over my head ;
Stretched out upon my old waterproof,
Dodging the raindrops from the roof.
Sing me to sleep in the camp fire's glow,
Munching French bread and jam, what ho !
Thinking of dear ones, and days long past,
Wond'ring how long this war will last.

CHORUS.

Far, far from star shells I long to be,
Those lights of home I'd much rather see ;
Thinking of dear ones away o'er the deep,
Waiting for someone to sing me to sleep.

NUMBER 50 ON THE LEAVE LIST.

Tune—" It's a long, long trail a-winding."

All night long you're feeling lonely
  When on sentry go,
And your feet are nearly frozen,
  Pacing to and fro ;
Then you think about the dear ones
  Safe asleep at home,
Nice and snug are they sleeping far away,
  And you give this gentle moan.

CHORUS.

It's a long, long time of waiting
  Until your turn comes for leave,
When you won't hear sergeants shouting
  " On the ropes, together, heave."
There'll be no more filling sandbags,
  And no more humping six-inch shells,
You'll be safe at home in Blighty drinking
  Whisky, rum, and Martell's.

UP AND DOWN

In February, 1918, a scheme was introduced for closer liaison between the Artillery and the Flying Corps in the Third Army. I was to spend a few days with "A" Flight, 15th Squadron R.F.C., while one of their officers was to spend a similar time with the Battery. Leaving the little Mess, with its spasmodic heating arrangements, one fine morning, I found myself in a comfortable Nissen hut, and was soon allotted a cubicle in the palatial sleeping quarters of the squadron. The Flight consisted of Captain Reeve, four or five pilots, and an equal number of observers. They were a jolly and hospitable lot of fellows, and at once made me feel quite at home. Three other flights, each with its own Mess and sleeping quarters, completed the Squadron.

At the Lechelle Aerodrome, just behind Ytres, we seemed quite out of the war, but that, perhaps, was because the nights were moonless, and the Boche H.V. gun was not at that time firing on the goods station. The morning after I arrived was " dud " for flying, and the weather conditions having been reported to the airmen by their batmen, the former turned over to sleep once more with a sigh of relief at having no early morning patrol to do. However, we spent an interesting and instructive morning looking round the aerodrome. This was my first opportunity of inspecting an aeroplane at close quarters. These machines were observation " 'buses " of the " R.E.8 " type, with the top plane longer than the bottom, a condition which gives greater stability, and it was with great relief that I learned the fact of their unsuitability for " stunting." They are good, serviceable machines, and have done most useful work, but they are slow both at flying and climbing. Here we also saw the latest addition to the Squadron, the Bristol fighter, which type was to replace the " R.E.8's," being a much better machine. At the time of writing, however, there still appear to be many " R.E.8's " in use.

After leaving the hangars we visited the Lecture Hall and saw with interest the Panoramic Ranging Board used in training pilots and observers. In size and detail it exceeded anything of the kind I had seen at Artillery training centres. The Photographic Section now attracted our attention. It appears the great art of aerial photography is to make a series of exposures in which the views do not overlap, but form a complete photograph of the area in question—a very difficult thing to do. Batteries received from this section their aerial photographs, often taken under difficult conditions, on clear days, by machines specially detailed for the work, which would often be interrupted by persistent enemy attacks. By midday the weather had cleared, and we replied in the affirmative when asked if we would like to go up for a " flip." I had the rather erroneous idea that I should be frozen stiff when I travelled skywards, but clad in a fur-lined boiler suit, cap, goggles, and sheepskin thigh-boots I experienced no discomfort from the cold. In this gear I climbed into the observer's compartment, and learnt, by the way, that the pilot and not the observer generally watches the fall of our rounds. The observer keeps his eyes skinned for Boche scouts, and works the machine-gun when necessary, but it is the duty of a man in charge of a slow observation machine of this type to avoid rather than seek a combat. My seat was somewhat like a revolving office stool, and within reach was the gun, also on a revolving frame, and having sights which are a marvel of ingenuity.

The critical moment arrived, and the mechanic began to turn the propeller by hand. At a certain stage both the pilot and the leading mechanic shouted " Contact ! " then the mechanic saluted and stepped smartly to the side. The propeller was now revolving with ever-increasing speed, and we started careering along the open field of the 'drome. Then the pilot manipulated his " joy-stick," the bumping ceased, and I realised that we were leaving *terra-firma*. We seemed to go straight ahead for some distance, when the plane made a sharp turn, and then began to " bank " in a most unmannerly style. I had been holding the sides of my compartment all the time pretty tightly, but I now took a firmer grip, and, catching my breath, uttered a fervent prayer and looked up at the sky. To tell the truth I was feeling in a rather topsy-turvy condition, for we were " banking " again, a performance which I had often watched

with interest from the ground ; but I can't honestly say
that I enjoyed taking part in the " real thing."

We had been going round in ever-increasing circles for
some time when the plane at last resumed a more or less
steady and normal course, and I began to take a " speir "
round. Our altitude was now about 2,500 to 3,000 feet,
and we were making, according to the speedometer, a speed
of about 60 miles an hour. Seen from above the ruined
villages seemed very close together, and roads, lanes and
railways seemed to dissect the country into large fields.
The noise of the engine and the rushing of the wind through
the planes was terrific. The pilot shouted to me that we
were just over Fins, and we then followed the road to
Gouzeaucourt, until we got to the battery position near
Tyke Dump, just off the sunken road to Heudicourt. I then
touched the pilot on the shoulder to let him know that we
were above the position, and he circled round and came down
lower. Our billets in the sunken road showed up plainly,
and there was no mistaking the gun-pits, but owing to the
heavy traffic round about, the fact that the pits were occu- ·
pied was not quite·so obvious as it otherwise might have
been. · They could, perhaps, have been taken for " dummy "
positions, or in conjunction with the disused pits near by,
for field fortifications. Anyhow the Boche had it well
" taped " on March 21st, so I·heard, but he paid no attention
to it while we were there.

My curiosity being satisfied, the pilot began to ascend
again. In front of us were beautiful white billowy clouds
at a height of about 3,500 feet, and we " banked " up
through these, until at length we came out on the upper side.
A glorious picture now revealed itself—the bright blue sky,
and the sun shining on the white clouds below, lighting them
up so that they resembled huge ice-bergs. Below again
where the clouds broke away loomed the earth in the far
distance.

At intervals the pilot pointed out to me objects of
interest. The whole trench system showed perfectly, like
huge scars, and shell-holes pock-marked the surface of the
ground. Really it made me think what " mugs " people
were to go anywere near the front line to do shoots on
trenches or strong points when such perfect observation

could be obtained from the air. Presently we saw below a huge heap of stones, which the pilot told me was Bapaume, and it was just then that he must have toyed with the " joy-stick," for the wretched machine put her nose straight down and we made a sheer drop of 2,000 feet at incredible speed. I have a vivid recollection of sitting well back on my stool with my arms and legs out straight, feeling that uncanny sensation associated with one's first descent in a lift. Seconds seemed like minutes, and I had just closed my eyes to await the final crash when the plane slid into a level course at about 2,000 feet, and followed the road home to the aerodrome. Vehicles and marching troops could be clearly discerned on the road, and at intervals I noticed that the altitude reading was less and less.

We soon reached the 'drome, round which we circled until the correct height and position for the final landing were gained. This operation of landing seems perfectly simple, but I understand it is one of the most difficult arts to acquire. Our trip had lasted three-quarters of an hour, but it seemed much longer, and except for the steep "banking " and sudden descent I had enjoyed it very much.

By the third day the other gunner and myself had become so content with aerodrome life that we tried hard to " wangle" a few extra days with the Squadron, and were both anxious to make another ascent. On this occasion I went up with a fellow-Yorkshireman about 11 a.m., and though the conditions were not particularly good, I enjoyed this better than my first trip. We went over the Gouzeaucourt position, and then made for the Hermies position, which I had not seen on my first flight. It was much more interesting than the one we occupied at the sunken road just mentioned. Two pits I could not distinguish at all, one pit was only just discernible, while the fourth showed up rather badly, owing, as I found out later, to the camouflage having come adrift ; otherwise I don't think I should have noticed it at all. An interesting view was obtained of the Drocourt switch, with the strong point of Quéant plainly visible. Our trip only lasted twenty minutes, and the pilot told me afterwards that it was a bad day for landing, and remarked on the unsteady flight of the machine, a fact which quite escaped my notice.

Unfortunately we were unable to prolong our stay, and in the Squadron tender I returned to the Battery, where I found the R.F.C. man just back from a visit to our O.P., " Bubble and Squeak." He, too, appeared to have enjoyed his stay with us, and after all a little variation adds an interest to life, especially army life.

" THE SKIPPER."

BATTERY HUMOUR

PHILIP, returning from a gay evening in the village, omits to salute a passing officer.

Officer : Are you aware that you should salute an officer ?

Philip : Beg pard'n, shir (*salutes with elaborate courtesy, which fairly takes the officer by surprise*).

Officer : Ve—very well, that will do.

Philip : Shir, are you aware that you haven't hic—knowledged my s'lute ?

BATH PARADE.

Enquiring Innocent : Will I take my towel, Sergeant-Major ?

Sergeant-Major : Well, what do you think ? Are you going to dry yourself in your blinkin' overcoat ?

AMMUNITION UP.

Horace : I—I really can't carry these shells, Corporal.

Jock : Dinna tell me ye canna carry shell ; I'll hae nane o' yer jookery-packery here !

HENENCOURT WOOD, 10.30 P.M.

1st Gunner : Come on, mate, turn out ; it's action.

2nd Gunner (new reinforcement) : No fear ! If I turn out once they'll be after me every night like this.

WHAT DID THE CAPTAIN REPLY ?

Scene—Wancourt. Dug-out doorway. A pitch-black night Pelting rain and high wind.

Captain (about to get the guns pulled in) : Have you a torch that you can let me have, Sergeant ?

Sergeant : No, sir, but I've got a few matches.

IN LIEU OF BREAD.

Irritated battery cook, having nothing but biscuits for tea ration, putting on the fire a piece of piano with hammers, keys, and wires attached. " Let the blarsted troops have music for tea."

CONDUCTIVITY.

Smythe : What's that noise on the 'phone over there ?

Juhyrst : Oh. only some silly fool outside kicking the wire.

J

RS/54Z/8. ENEMY CARRIER PIGEONS.

" Batteries are to open fire on these birds only when they are flying towards the front line."

SUB——DIVISION.

Officer : How many o' ye's in that dug-oot ?
Corporal : Nine, sir.
Officer : Well, come oot, the half o' ye.

A FAT LOT.

Army Order received when the battery had been on iron rations about three weeks.
" Dripping must be collected in tins and forwarded at the end of each month to rail head."
Reply.—" Up to the present no dripping has been extracted from the bully beef on which the battery has been living for three weeks."

NOVEMBER 11TH, 1918.

1st Girl : I think it's such a pity the war didn't last till Xmas.
2nd Girl : Why ?
1st Girl : Well, you see, I've saved £95, and by that time I should have just got the hundred.

THE PEN IS MIGHTIER THAN THE SWORD.

Scene—Demicourt. Time, 7 p.m., November 30th, 1917. Sergeant-Major superintending the withdrawal of the guns after one of the worst days in the history of the battery. Resumption of enemy bombardment probable at any moment.
Signaller : Mr. D——t has just rung through to ask if you will find his writing-pad and send it down.
S.M.—Can't stop now.
Despatch Rider (later) : I've just come from billets, and Mr. D——t told me to ask you for his writing-pad.
S.M. : Don't know anything about his d——d writing pad.
Officer's Servant (later) : When you come down will you bring Mr. D——t's writing-pad ?
S.M. : Oh, —— Mr. D——t and his —— writing-pad.

DUD ?

Officer : Hello, Balloon. Did you see my last shot ?
Balloon : No burst observed near your target, sir.
Officer : Well, er—er, it must have gone somewhere else.

The Delicacy.

Old Hand : Come along, we'll go and get our tea now, and have it together in the dug-out.

Reinforcement (one week in France) : Thank you very much. You know I've just found a tin of corned beef which will do nicely for tea.

The Flowers that Bloom in the Spring.

Officer : Put on your steel hat and gas-mask and go to the gardens in Wancourt and get me some roses for the officers' mess table to-night.

His Servant : But, sir, I——

Officer : Do as I tell you, and don't argue.

His Servant : Well, sir, I have a little boy at home, and when he says " What did you do in the great war, daddy ? " won't I look a fool if I say " Gathered flowers for the officers' mess."

THE INDENT

(To the tune of " Solomon Levy.")

Note.—For the benefit of the uninitiated it should perhaps be mentioned that G.1098 is the official list of all the stores a fully-equipped battery should possess.

There's dozens of things have gone astray in chasing after
    Fritz,
And a lot of the stuff that hasn't been lost the shells have knocked
    to bits ;
So now I'm making a lengthy list before it gets too late
And running my finger up and down the G. ten-ninety-eight.

CHORUS.

Oh, pity the Quarter, pity the Quarter bloke ;
    Oh, pity the Quarter, pity the Quarter bloke.
I'm making a list of all I've lost before it gets too late,
And finding the horrible names of things in G. ten-ninety-eight.

There's scotches, skids, and spokeshaves, and a couple of sel-
    vagees,
A lump of Chatterton's compound and the four good swingle-
    trees ;
An obturator adjusting disc, and the linch-pins bracketed
    (" spare "),
Clinometer springs, and bolts and nuts with countersunk head
    that's square.
    Oh, pity the Quarter, &c.

There's twenty yards of flannelette beside the hemp undressed,
And gun-wheel mats and marline spikes to bring the Hows to rest ;
There's wrenches, bits, and borers, and the things that look like
    quilts ;
Whatever we miss we mustn't forget the battery's wadmiltilts.
    Oh, pity the Quarter, &c.

And boards and buckets, binoculars and a carborundum stone,
With pins and pipes and pliers and pouch to suit the telephone ;
Electric " gadgets " and flexible leads for piquet lamps at the
    back,
Some soap and tallow, and potash and resin, and sal-ammoniac.
    Oh, pity the Quarter, &c.

The girdles and the handspikes and the limbers ; in the rush
I'd nearly forgotten to mention here the piasaba brush ;
The hurricane lamp and grindstone, and the tinman's little pot,
The stable barrows and dubbin and grease,, and that must be
    the lot.
    Oh, pity the Quarter, &c.

                          " 154151."

LIMERICKS

There was a young officer, he
Ordered battery fire at O.P.,
   When he shouted, " By gosh !
   I have slain forty Boche,"
The fact was he'd *nearly* hit three.

There once was a canteen. No doubt
You have heard there were such things about ;
   But this I do know
   When I used to go
The stuff they had in was sold out.

There was a young soldier called Goff,
At bayonet drill he would scoff ;
   Told to " Fix," silly kid,
   That's just what he did ;
The sergeant, of course, ticked him off.

There was a young smoker who'd been
In Flanders since nineteen-fourteen ;
   They offered him bags
   Of the best sort of fags,
But he said, " I prefer Ruby Queen."

There was an old chap who said " Thanks,"
And swigged till he reeled in the ranks ;
   " He ought," folk would say,
   " Not to be R.G.A.,
He should have joined up in the Tanks."

There was a long time without mail,
And the battery sent up a wail ;
   " Why not try," said a wag,
   " To put by a good bag,
And issue it when the posts fail ? "

There once was a cook that said " Who
Would like a few ' spuds ' in his stew ? "
   But he gave with his wrist
   A peculiar twist,
And *no* " taters " reached me or you.

RHONDDA

YES, food control—that's my strong point. Give me a small pan of stew and a big ladle, and I'll see that the troops don't go hungry. Ur-a, Ur-a. Two Machonochies, three tins of bully, and water—good pump water with a pinch of salt in it, and I'll guarantee to act fair by the troops, mate. Here it is, just off the fire. Good clear stuff like this you wouldn't get in England. *One*—hold your dixie up, mate, or else I can't get it all in. *Two*—sorry to keep you waiting, Bill, and all that, but I *know* your bean is somewhere in this stew. No, old man—(*that's three*) I'm sorry, but I must tip that little potato back again. There's others to come, you know. If I let a bit too much like that go into the wrong dixie—*four*—I go all of a tremble, and get sharp stabbing pains in my stomach. Oh, no, you can't expect meat—*four*—when it's all boiled to gravy. No good grumbling at me, is it now? You better see Sir Douglas Haig or some of the 'eds about it. I *got* to make it go round. *Five*. Wait a minute, have this drip off the ladle. Ur-a, Ur-a. *Six*. No, old man, it won't run to more than two bits of carrot—heart's good and all that, but I counted the bits this morning. *Six*.

* * * * * * *

Fifty-five—Fifty-six—Fifty-seven. All very well to say *House*, mate, you ought to have my job. No, that isn't meat, it's my jack-knife—fell in just now. *Fifty-nine*.

* * * * * * *

Seventy-two. Put a drop of hot water in, Bob, and give it a stir, there's three more to come. *Seventy-three, Seventy-four*—no, it isn't very thick to-day—got no meal you know. *Seventy-five*. Well, that's done with. What! five more! I must have counted wrong. Very sorry and all that, Ur-a, Ur-a, but you better ask Frank for five tins of bully.

" Y."

ÇA NE FAIT RIEN

To the tune of " Comin' thro' the Rye."

If your slacks are very ragged,
   San-affairy-ann.
If your putties' edge is jagged,
   San-affairy-ann.
If your tunic's all to tatters,
Patch it if you can ;
But if you can't, why let it rip, say
   San-affairy-ann.

If new shirts are not forthcomin',
   San-affairy-ann.
If the Quarter's not got some in,
   San-affairy-ann.
If the battery's short of *savon,*
Try another plan,
And turn the old one inside out, it's
   San-affairy-ann.

Though 'twas sometimes hard to stick it,
   San-affairy-ann.
By-and-by we'll get our ticket,
   San-affairy-ann.
Though the ordnance stores are empty,
   We don't care a ——,
We'll start for home in nowt but pants, and
   San-affairy-ann.

MORE SOUVENIRS

Zum Bahnhof, to the railway station. *Achtung Eisenbahn,* warning, railway. *Zum Feld-lazarett,* to Field Hospital. *Das Rauchen ist verboten,* no smoking. *Nach Lille,* to Lille. *Kein Eingang,* no entrance. *Flugplatz,* aviation ground. *Belegung,* billet. *Unterstand,* underground shelter. *Trinkwasser,* drinking water. *Wasser Abkochen,* cookingwater. *Ortskommandantur,* Town-Major. *Ausgang,* Exit. *Eintritt verboten,* entry forbidden. *Munitions-Lager,* Ammunition dump. *Bahnubergang,* level crossing. *Hochspannung, Vorsicht, Lebensgefahr,* high tension electricity, warning, danger.

TELLMANISM

" Our object is not merely to teach you, but to teach you to teach yourself."

THE triumphant progress of the Tellman system continues. All ranks, from Acting Unpaid Supernumerary Gunners to Field Marshals, are rushing to enrol. Consider calmly whether as a Tellmanist you could not do better than you are doing now. Below are a few extracts from letters recently received. Originals may be seen at the office by anyone interested.

SPRUCER.—" The claims you make for your system are too modest. The improvement in my memory is marvellous. I can now remember being present at battles which took place before I left England. Your chapter on the Five Branches of Bullpeddling is invaluable."

LEADSWINGER.—" Before I had finished the first little grey book I ' wangled ' a special leave, and since returning I have had much greater success when describing to the doctor the horrible pain that I haven't got in my stomach."

STUDENT.—" When I started in the French class I thought I should never learn to *parley-voo*, but now I am getting on *très bon*, and even Mr. Loftus can hardly follow me. It comes so natural that I say " *Bon centime* " without thinking, when I take my glass of *vin blanc*. It is doubtful whether I shall ever speak English properly again, Monsieur Tellman. *Bon jour.*"

H. CLENCH.—" Tellmanism means success. I never did so well in a whist drive before. Since becoming a Tellmanist I have been demobilised completely, leaving those who have not taken your course behind at Phalempin."

ACTING UNPAID BOMBARDIER.—" There is no doubt as to the value of your course to the ambitious man. I feel sure that as promotions go at present I shall, by constant Tellmanising, be Sergeant-Major of my battery before peace is signed."

J. MUIR.—" The efficiency of my flyproofing has increased 50 per cent. Your course is worth its weight in gold."

N. O. JOB.—" My prospects on leaving the army were very poor until I read your advertisements. Now I feel certain that I shall do well with a tray of matches and bootlaces."

M. O'HARA.—" I can now get the ' Numbers One ' out in record time. Every evening the little grey books are read in the Sergeants' Mess——if there is no beer in the canteen."

H. O. LYDFORD.—" I took the Tellman course because ' changing guard ' was not done satisfactorily. Instead of a duty the work of Orderly Officer has now become a fascinating pastime."

RATION BOMBARDIER.—" The Tellman course soon makes it clear that ' the impossible is possible, and the unattainable is attainable,' as one of your students so aptly puts it. This information would have been another boon to the battery in the days of bully and biscuit. I wish I had taken your course earlier."

A. KING.—" Since completing your course I find the canteen profits have gone up by leaps and bounds, and my memory for prices and faces is almost perfect."

W. N. BATES (Air Scout).—"Anyone who gives the course a fair trial will never blow the ' stand fast ' for one of our own planes."

H. PUNTON (Despatch Rider).—" My work in the army often makes it necessary to be in two places at once. Reading your advertisements induces me to believe that I can manage this feat. I hope to halve my work by taking the course."

AMMUNITION BOMBARDIER.—"The severest strain to which I have put your system has been in making up the ammunition report ; but after reading all the little books through once forwards and twice backwards the Sergeant-Major (another hardened Tellmanist) and myself managed to account for all the rounds but 73, which we must have left with 3 Siege. No person who has not served in a battery can appreciate the value of this testimonial, and nothing but Tellmanism could have coped with the problem. All my twelve children are taking your course."

A. D. V. T.

"VULCAN"

EARLY one cold wintry morning in January, 1917, a telephonist and I, heavily laden with sundry instruments of
observation and telephones, left the billets at Anzin for
our first twelve hours' duty at the chimney O.P., " Vulcan,"
in Arras. A few signallers had already been up this chimney, and naturally had made the most of their achievement
in the half-whispered stories with which they successfully
put the " wind up " the remainder of the men who had to
follow them on observation duty. With these hair-raising
tales still fresh in our minds we passed through the gates
of Arras, speculating as to whether unconsciousness followed
or preceded a fall from a great height. Passing along the
Rue de Gambetta we reached the square in front of the
station, and beheld the famous " Vulcan " looming up
through the morning mist. In a spirit of apparent un-
concern, something between resigned bravado and " windy "
sang froid, we approached our post of duty by way of the
water tower which lay across the contorted railway lines.
As we unloaded our paraphernalia a coin was produced
to decide who should ascend first, but our officer settled
the argument when he requested me to go up and report
on the visibility.

The well of the chimney was reached by descending
a manhole near the base, and entering a small pitch-dark
passage, at the end of which a view of the interior could be
obtained. Iron staples were fixed at regular intervals in
the smutty wall for climbing purposes, while a rope which
gently swayed to and fro was used for pulling up instruments, rations, and overcoats. As I mentioned before, the
morning was cold—intensely so—and in my excitement
I had forgotten to bring my gloves, but I only discovered
their need when I had climbed about 20 steps. Round
each rung was a thin coating of ice, and my hands soon
became numbed with the cold, but after warming them one
at a time I continued. About 40 feet up I noticed a shaft
of light shining through the darkness, and imagined I had
reached the top, but this light proved to be coming through

a ragged shell-hole where the chimney had suffered a direct hit. If you have ever tried climbing up the wrong side of a ladder you will realise that it was impossible for the climber to relax his hold for an instant in ascending the tapering chimney. At this juncture the heavy breathing from below confirmed my suspicions that I was being followed, and the somewhat strained language told me that my progress was unnecessarily slow. I put a " jerk " in it, and completed the 114 steps to the first platform, and, lying on the wooden floor, watched the others ascend. "Are we near the top ? " said a husky voice, and by way of revenge I answered in the negative.

The Engineers had erected two platforms at the top of the chimney, one for telephonists and the higher one for observation purposes. Bricks had been removed from the side, and through the aperture, which afforded a splendid view of the Scarpe Valley, a watch was kept on enemy movement. About an hour after ascending the officer communicated with the Battery, reporting movement on the Arras-Beaurains road, and later a registration shoot was carried through on a cross-roads.

By dinner-time we had more or less become used to the dizzy height, and enjoyed the novel experience of being steeple-jacks, but the breeze which sprang up in the early afternoon tested our nerve. With each gust of wind the chimney was slightly rocked, and momentarily I expected the structure to topple over, but the telephonist on the lower deck seemed quite at home as he sat reading his " Union Jack."

When visibility had become too poor for observation, we received " C.I." from the Battery, and descended the chimney, making our way back through Arras to partake of hot tea and enjoy a well-earned rest.

" STEVE."

ANY SOLDIER TO HIS SON

What did you do, daddy, in the great world war ?
Well, I learned to peel potatoes and to scrub the barrack
  floor,
I learned to use a shovel, and a barrow, and a pick,
I learned to "get a jerk on," and I learned to "make 'em
  click."
I learned the road to Folkestone, and I looked my last on
  home,
As I heaved my beans and bacon to the fishes and the foam ;
And the Blighty boats went by us, and the harbour hove in
  sight,
And they landed us and sorted us, and marched us " By the
  right
Quick-march ! " along the cobbles, by the kids who ran along
Singing "Appoo—Spearmante—Shokolah " through dingy old
  Boulong.
And the widows, and the nurses, and the niggers and Chinese,
And the gangs of smiling Fritzes, as saucy as you please.
I learned to ride, as soldiers ride, from Etaps to the Line,
For days and nights in cattle-trucks, packed in like droves of
  swine.
I learned to curl and kip it on a foot of muddy floor,
And to envy cows and horses that have beds of " beaucoup "
  straw.
I learned to wash in shell-holes, and to shave myself in tea,
While the fragments of a mirror did a balance on my knee.
I learned to dodge the whizzbangs, and the flying lumps· of
  lead,
And to keep a foot of earth between the sniper and my
  head.
I learned to keep my haversack well filled with buckshee food ;
To take the Army issue and to pinch what else I could.
I learned to cook Maconochie with candle ends and string,
With " four-by-two " and sardine oil and any god-dam thing.
I learned to use my bayonet according as you please
For a breadknife or a chopper, or a prong for toasting cheese.
I learned to gather souvenirs, that home I hoped to send,
And hump them round for months and months and dump them
  in the end.
I learned to hunt for vermin in the lining of my shirt,
To crack them with my finger-nail and feel the beggars
  spurt.
I learned to sleep by snatches on the firestep of a trench,
And to eat my breakfast mixed with mud and Fritz's heavy
  stench.

I learned to pray for Blighty ones, and lie and squirm with
fear
When Gerry started strafing and the Blighty ones were near.
I learned to write home cheerful with my heart a lump of lead,
With the thought of you and mother when she heard that I was
dead.
And the only thing like pleasure over there I ever knew
Was to hear my pal come shouting " There's a parcel, mate, for
you."
So much for what I did do : now for what I have not done.
Well, I never kissed a French girl, and I never killed a Hun ;
I never missed an issue of tobacco, pay, or rum,
I never made a friend, and yet I never lacked a chum.
I never used to grumble after breakfast in the Line
That the eggs were cooked too lightly or the bacon cut too fine.
I never told a sergeant just exactly what I thought ;
I never did a pack drill, for I never quite got caught.
I never stopped a whizzbang, though I've stopped a lot of
mud,
But the one which Fritz sent over with my name on was a dud.
I never played the hero or walked about on top,
I kept inside my funkhole when the shells began to drop ;
Well, Tommy Jones's father must be made of different stuff :
I never asked for trouble, the issue was enough.
So I learned to live and lump it in the lovely land of war,
Where all the face of Nature seems a monstrous septic
sore ;
Where the bowels of earth hang open, like the guts of something
slain,
And the rot and wreck of everything are churned and churned
again ;
Where all is done in darkness and where all is still in day ;
Where living men are buried and the dead unburied lay ;
Where men inhabit holes like rats, and only rats live there,
Where cottage stood and castle once in days before La Guerre ;
Where endless files of soldiers thread the everlasting way,
By endless miles of duckboards, through endless walls of clay.
Where life is one hard labour, and a soldier gets his rest
When they leave him in the daisies with a puncture in his
chest.
And I read the Blighty papers, where the warriors of the pen
Tell of " Christmas in the trenches," and " The Spirit of our
Men."
And I saved the choicest morsels, and I read them to my chum,
And he muttered, as he cracked a louse and wiped it off his
thumb :
" May a thousand chats from Belgium crawl their fingers as
they write ;
May they dream they're not exempted till they faint with mortal
fright ;

May the fattest rats in Dickebusch race over them in bed ;
May the lies they've written choke them like a gas cloud till
    they're dead ;
May the horror and the torture and the things they never tell
(For they only write to order) be reserved for them in Hell ! "

           *   *   *   *   *   *   *   *

You'd like to be a soldier, and go to France some day ?
By all the dead in Delville Wood, by all the nights I lay
Between our line and Fritz's, before they brought me in ;
By this old wood and leather stump, that once was flesh and
    skin ;
By all the lads who crossed with me but never crossed again ;
By all the prayers their mothers and their sweethearts prayed
    in vain ;
Before the things that were that day should ever more befall,
May God, in common pity, destroy us one and all !

        *   *   *   *   *   *   *   *

Printed in the United Kingdom
by Lightning Source UK Ltd.
116070UKS00001B/6